SO-AHS-041

SALES MADE EASY:
62 STRATEGIES THAT WORK

BY
LARRY A. BAUMAN

COLUMBA PUBLISHING COMPANY, INC.
AKRON, OHIO 44313

Sales Made Easy: 62 Strategies That Work
by Larry A. Bauman

Published by Columba Publishing Co. Inc.
Akron, Ohio USA
Copyright 2001 Larry A. Bauman
All rights reserved
Manufactured in the United States of America
ISBN 0-938655-86-8

Editor
Sheri Leigh Galat

10 9 8 7 6 5 4 3 2 1

Translation or reproduction of any part of this work, beyond that permitted by the International Copyright Act, without the permission of the copyright owner, is unlawful. Please request permission or further information from the Permissions Department, Columba Publishing Co. Inc., 2003 West Market Street, Akron, OH 44313, USA. Telephone: 1.330.836.2619 Fax: 1.330.836.9659.

The information contained in this publication is based on the personal experiences and opinions of Larry A. Bauman. The suggestions are offered in good faith, but without guarantee, because methods of persons are beyond our control. We recommend the user determine, for her/his own purposes, the suitability of all materials and suggestions mentioned. Columba Publishing Co., Larry A. Bauman, and the other contributors disclaim all responsibility for loss or damage resulting from the use of information furnished within.

The quotes which introduce each topic were selected by the author to illustrate his own personal views. Inclusion of quotes in this book does not imply endorsement from the quoted authors or their estates.

B868 $14.95

TABLE OF CONTENTS

MANAGING
YOUR
BUSINESS

PROLOGUE

A man on a camel rode through miles of the sun-drenched desert searching for some sign of life. His supplies were running low when his camel died. Now on foot, he desperately sought refuge from the heat, and, most importantly, a source for water. Suddenly, he came across a salesman in the middle of the desert.

"Thank God I found you!" the man cried. "Please help me. I'm in dire need of some water."

"Well," said the salesman, "I don't have any water. But would you like to buy one of these fine ties?"

"What am I going to do with a tie?" the man asked.

"That's what I'm selling sir. If you don't like it, I can't help you."

The man left the salesman and walked on for many more miles, praying each minute that he would find refuge from the scorching sun. His eyes had squinted a hundred times when he saw a restaurant in the distance. Unable to comprehend a restaurant located in the middle of the desert, he assumed the place was a mirage, but decided to check it out anyway. As he approached the door, his mouth opened in amazement—it was real. The restaurant actually existed.

The doorman stopped him before he entered.

"I must have some water," the man mouthed to the doorman.

"I am sorry, sir," the doorman said, "but you can't come in here without a tie!"

Now, I ask you, did this salesman do his job?

ACCOUNT CLASSIFICATION

A prudent question is one-half of wisdom.
- Francis Bacon

Making sure your customer is properly classified is very important. There are several reasons why you should pay close attention to this small detail.

1. The customer's buying discount is usually tied directly to the classification.
2. Materials being mailed are sent out by account classification.
3. Some products should not be sold to certain classifications.
4. Certain classifications produce more company profits than others.
5. Incentive bonuses may be directly tied to customer classification.
6. Buying programs are designed with account classification in mind.
7. The time allotment for your sales call is driven by the type of account on which you are calling.

If a customer is improperly classified, it can cost you sales. In today's marketplace, it seems every retail framing account does some corporate business. This does not necessarily make the account an OEM. But it does raise the question of whether the account is classified correctly and is receiving the proper buying discounts.

Classifications are a useful tool for the salesperson.

Making sure each customer is classified properly is your responsibility. You have to make that determination in the field. It is not the responsibility of office personnel to make the determination for you.

Account lists should be reviewed regularly. If changes need to be made, your company should have a procedure in place to make sure this is done quickly and efficiently. Take the time to review your account listings. It does make a difference to both you and your account.

CALL DOCUMENTATION

Nothing is a waste of time if you use the experience wisely.
- Auguste Rodin

When I got my first sales job, I was trained in the style of the day by riding with the company's most successful rep and carrying his cases for a week. I was young, green, and eager to make a good impression with my teacher, so I asked probably more than your average number of questions. At one point during the first couple of days, I asked Ike "How do you organize yourself?" He told me to reach into his briefcase and take out the plastic chicken. I did so, not knowing what I was getting myself into. I pulled this yellow, plastic chicken from the case and it was covered with signatures. He said: "You see that? Every time one of my customers places an order with me, he gets to sign the chicken. I'm on my fourth chicken because I wore the first three out getting signatures." I must tell you, some of the signatures were in very auspicious places.

The point was, he had a way to document most calls he made, and if memory serves me correctly, he wrote an order at every stop that week. Though a bit unconventional, his system worked well for him until he had too many plastic chickens to fit into the car with all his samples.

Many salespeople run their business from their front shirt pocket. How many times have you seen a person who, when asked for information, pulls a huge wad of papers from their front shirt pocket to refer to some handwritten note made on a napkin in a restaurant? I tried this for a while, but I found I inevitably lost important notes or names. So I moved on to a written "daytimer" personal organizer system.

Today, most call documentation is done through sales automation of some sort. With the advent of laptop computers, most companies have put their sales forces on-line to help them manage the huge overflow of information that is available today. We are exposed to 300 times more information today than we were exposed to in 1995. What is even scarier, that amount of exposure is expected to increase another 300 times by 2005. Is it any wonder that we have a hard time remembering Wilbur's wife's name from a call made only two days ago? The need for a quick and efficient contact management system was born.

Small electronic organizers are everywhere today, being used in all walks of life. Having this large amount of information readily available has made the life of the salesperson much easier. A quick handwritten note goes immediately into a file that can be recalled instantly. Expenses don't get lost. Orders can be immediately downloaded to a company mainframe without having to be rewritten or copied. The entire life history of your customers, from birthdays to reorder dates can be managed effectively and easily.

Methods of call documentation will become more important as the amount of information we need to keep increases. You will have to determine which method is best for you. But, regardless of how the information is recorded, making sure it gets recorded is most important. Whether you use handwritten notes or an electronic organizer or a laptop computer, record your information somewhere, and refer to it before you walk through your customer's door. You will feel better about your call and, I promise, so will your customer.

CELEBRATING SUCCESS

All you need in this life is ignorance and confidence,
and the success is sure.
- Samuel L. Clemens

I once had a salesman tell me he missed working for a company that liked to celebrate successes. At his previous job, the sales manager would send out a short list each week of individual successes that had worked in the market. This was a computer company that was growing by leaps and bounds at the time. When the salesman mentioned the idea to me, I felt that because our company was currently managing a defensive market position this approach would not be successful. How wrong I was.

Today, people usually stay with a job for job satisfaction. This can include the amount of money they make, quality of the company with regard to services or products, or individual recognition that is provided to them. I was surprised to learn that most of us don't care as much about the money aspect of the job as the recognition given on an individual level. The words "you're doing a great job" can go a long way toward getting us to the next plateau. When money is attached, the reward becomes even sweeter.

Achievement awards are an important part of every company. They come in many forms. IBM used to have a steak and beans dinner. Those individuals who made their quota for the year got to eat steak, those who didn't had to eat beans. I'm sure it made for an interesting sales meeting. I know that if I had to eat beans for dinner one year, there would be no way I would be a part of that the next year.

I once had a sales consultant call on me to try to sell me his abilities as a motivational speaker for sales training. He started the conversation by asking what motivated me and how did I hire my salespeople. I told him I was money-motivated and I wanted the same type of salespeople working for me. He sat back and said the following: "You can motivate people in three ways, with money, fear, and attitude. All three can work, but all successful managers use the last one, attitude motivation, to be the most successful." He was right and I have never forgotten his words to me, even though he didn't get the job.

Small achievements add up to big achievements. This is true in all aspects of our lives, at work, at home, your family, your health. Make your own list. Take some time to look at your successes on a variety of levels. Daily successes turn into weekly, weekly successes turn into monthly, etc., etc. Tell somebody about them. Blow your own horn a little. You deserve it. And when somebody tells you about their successes, revel in it with them. Celebrate them. The world needs more successes in every respect. Make sure you do your part to provide a few of your own.

CRUNCH TIME

The years teach much which the days never know.
- Ralph Waldo Emerson

I had a salesperson tell me the other day "It's crunch time." What a great way to describe the winter holiday season. When I think of "crunch time," I always revert back to college years when a term paper was due or cramming for a midterm or final was at hand. I hadn't really associated it with business. But the more I thought about it, the more I thought it was appropriate to use as a business term.

The framing industry has a seasonal business cycle. In the course of the year, the third and fourth quarters are the time when retailers are the busiest, and hopefully when they make the most money. These quarters do not necessarily run on a calendar year. I had a retailer explain to me not long ago that his fourth quarter ran from November through January. Regardless of which months you choose, six are usually good and the other six are usually somewhat mediocre.

As a salesperson, you should look at your market and calculate when your "crunch time" begins and ends. Every market is different. Awareness of the market pulse can help you produce the results you require to be successful in the marketplace. If you miss the optimum buying time, your production can be affected for at least a month, —at the worst, it can ruin your year.

By determining when your crunch time is, you can schedule your personal time as well as your business time to get the most rewards. Obviously, there is no substitute for working hard all the time. But if you are able to work hard and smart, your benefits will the greater. Know your crunch time. Your sales performance will be greatly enhanced by paying attention to this important detail.

FACING THE FUTURE

The wise man must remember that while he is a descendant of the past,
he is a parent of the future.
- Herbert Spencer

One of my year-end projects is writing down my goals for the coming year. I've done this for the past ten years and it has become a real barometer of what I get accomplished on a yearly basis in all aspects of my life. I have to admit there are certain areas each year where I fall short of my goals, but on the other hand, there are many things that do get accomplished, which makes me feel pretty good. I am able to recognize my progress because I can look at a written record of my goals.

All the seminars say to make your goals very specific and measurable. They say this for one reason and one reason only: it's the best way. When I first started doing this, I had some very general goals that were somewhat unspecific and certainly not measurable. When I sit down to analyze how I am measuring up during the year, I find it is the overly general goals on which I have made little or no progress. You may want to re-write your list of goals several times until it is short, concise and described in terms that can be measured. The old adage "less is more" applies here.

The hardest part of putting your goals in writing is getting it done the first time. Many goals can stay the same from year to year, such as "eat less red meat on a weekly basis" or "exercise regularly each week." Others are more far-reaching, such as preparing for retirement or financing a college education. Many goals play off of one another;

one cannot be accomplished without first completing another.

I like to divide my goals into specific areas. Here are the areas in which I set goals every year:

- Financial
- Health
- Business
- Personal
- Community
- Spiritual

There are other categories you may decide to use, but these have worked for me. I can usually slot every goal I have under one of these general categories.

Volkswagen has a commercial that talks about two kinds of people, those who drive and those who don't: drivers wanted. Achieving your goals is important to your own personal well being. I encourage you to take a few minutes at the end of this year and think about what you want to accomplish in the coming year, then write it down. Review it regularly. It will help keep you on track. You will be surprised and feel good about what you have achieved at the end of the year.

WHAT'S GROWING IN THE BOOT?

*The significant problems we face cannot be solved by the
same level of thinking that created them.*
- Albert Einstein

Most cars have trunks (although many vehicles today do not, due to the popularity of SUV's and minivans.) If you have a car in England, the Brits refer to the trunk as a "boot." Whatever you call the storage area of your vehicle, it can be a valuable tool when you are on the road. If organized correctly, it can do much more than hold your luggage—it can become a mini-office that provides the materials necessary for making a good sales call.

Samples should always go in the trunk. I had a salesperson call me one time and tell me "Hey, I've got a guy who wants to buy the whole line." I said "Great, who is it?" and he said "I don't know, but he took every sample case I had last night out of my car." I would have enjoyed seeing the thief's face when he opened the case to find moulding samples. Not only was the loss of the cases a nuisance, it was also costly to the company and the salesperson, even though it did provide a good story.

Tight organization with marked cases provides quick reference when a specific product is needed for the sales presentation. Organization can be quickly accomplished with a tape measure and masking tape. Measure your trunk and outline the measurements with masking tape in a clean, flat area of your home. Try several configurations until you achieve the best use of your trunk space. Don't forget that easy access is very important to good organization in your trunk.

Once the sample cases are arranged, you will see how

much additional space is available for collateral materials: luggage, tools for the car, etc. If you compartmentalize your trunk with boxes or plastic carriers from the local container store, finding price lists and other printed material can be quick and easy.

What should go in your boot? At the risk of sounding like Martha Stewart, here are a few suggestions. Sorry, no golf clubs.

- Samples cases
- Literature boxes with dividers
- Desk tools such as a stapler, pens, scotch tape, paper clips, etc.
- First Aid Kit
- One quart of water (for drinking or overheated radiators)
- Car tools (don't forget the duct tape)
- Cold weather survival kit (not needed in all climates)
- Road reflectors

When I first got married, my wife let a friend borrow her car for a few days. The car was returned in good shape, full of gas and my wife never bothered to check the trunk. A few weeks later, she went to put groceries in the trunk. When she opened it, a small field of oats sprang out. Unknown to my wife, her friend had used the car to buy oats for her horses and the bag had spilled. In the meantime, moisture from rain had gotten in the trunk and made the oats sprout and grow. Everyone got a good laugh out of the situation. The point of the story is that trunks should be used as a tool. My wife's friend had used the trunk as a tool, but neglected to put it back in good order when she finished.

An organized trunk makes your road life easier. Take the time to do it; it is well worth the effort.

DEALING WITH INCLEMENT WEATHER

It's raining on the enemy too.
- Dwight D. Eisenhower

One of my favorite places to work is California. Inevitably, the weather there is warm and sunny, while back in Chicago there always seems to be some type of lousy weather happening. In truth, bad weather happens to all of us, even those living in California (just less frequently.) I have always wondered about the effect of bad weather on the salesperson out making calls. Does battling the elements make him or her more successful? Less successful? How should the salesperson approach bad weather and what are the benefits of being out during that time?

If a salesperson calls me and says there is ice and two feet of snow, and asks me "What should I do?" my answer is: use your own judgement. Don't do anything foolish, because you want to live to sell another day. But if you can get out, those customers who have forged through the bad weather to get to their shops really appreciate a salesperson who has made the same effort. This often opens doors that have previously been closed.

When you walk through the door and the customer says "What are you doing out in this weather?", my standard reply has always been: "It's a great day for ducks and salespeople." I usually substitute some other appropriate animal for cold weather, like a penguin. More often than not, the customers agree and show their approval by taking extra time with the salesperson, maybe even placing a larger order than usual.

Customers appreciate that extra effort. Your company appreciates that extra effort. But the final decision about making sales calls in bad weather always lies with you. My advice: always err on the side of caution. That gives you the opportunity to remain safe and in good health for yourself, for your family, and for future business opportunities for you and your company.

INCREASING YOUR PROFIT

Don't go around saying the world owes you a living;
the world owes you nothing; it was here first.
- Samuel Clemens

All businesses are looking for ways to increase profits, and field salespeople should be no different, because they are an integral part of the business structure. Often salespeople focus solely on the gross sales (how much you sold) versus the net sales (how much money you made). Both are important and both are increasingly connected to the success of both the salesperson and the overall health of the company.

What is profit? Profit is what remains after all expenses are paid. Some things that affect profit are within your control. On the other hand, some are beyond your control.

There are four critical areas which play a part in the profit made from your sales:
1. The prices charged for the products you sell. Pricing plays a strategic part in the profit equation. "Loss leaders," products sold at or below cost, are one example. These products are priced to unload overstock or tempt the customer to buy, but they are not profitable. To yield a profit from a loss leader sale, the salesperson must sell additional products to the customer.
2. The amount or volume of the products you sell. A product priced with a narrow profit margin can become a profitable sale if a large quantity is purchased. On the flip side, a salesperson could sell less product this month than last month, but show higher

profit, because the products sold this month were simply more profitable.

3. Variable costs incurred as a result of selling, such as travel expenses. You have some control of these costs.
4. Fixed costs, which do not change regardless of whether your sales go up or go down. Example: your car payment or car allowance, the monthly rent on your office. You have no immediate control over these costs because they are established by your employer or by contract.

All businesses look for ways to improve their profits. The trap most fall into is focusing on price as a single profit generator. Just as with any business, a strategy needs to be developed to monitor and improve the profit yielded from a sales territory. With this in mind, any profit improvement must focus on either or both of two things:

1. Achieving a higher gross margin per dollar of sales by increasing sales and/or reducing variable costs.
2. Achieving greater sales per dollar of fixed costs by increasing productivity of those items that have a fixed cost.

If you work on a salary plus commission, you are both a fixed cost and a variable cost for your company. What are you doing to make yourself and the company more profitable?

MAKE A LIST

Do not be too timid and squeamish about your actions.
All life is an experiment.
- Ralph Waldo Emerson

When the winter holidays are upon us, we all make out our lists for those special gifts we want to give. Mine, this year, is actually printed out from the computer. This could mean a few things:

1. My list is too long to keep in my head.
2. It is too long to write by hand (I usually can't read my own writing anyway.)
3. My list is a combination of other lists that I have saved over the course of the year with ideas for each person.

Have you ever been accused of keeping lists of lists? The most recognized list for me is the daily "to do" list. I also keep a weekly and a monthly list of things I need to accomplish in every part of my life, whether it centers on work, home, health, social, or financial. A list is my way of mapping out the day and making sure that everything I want to accomplish can be checked off at some point.

Depending on the type of person you are, you may want to use color to highlight, grade, or prioritize your list. Some people like to use symbols to code their lists. Some lists work well because they are considered linear. One item leads to the next and that one leads to the next and so on. Other lists are more fluid and present more of a challenge to finish or execute each item. My Saturday lists are a good example of this type of list. I usually write the list in a James Joyce manner, stream of consciousness, with little planning other than to get the items accomplished.

A planned "to do" list can make the day flow much better than my "Saturday list" format. My lists for work-related matters are always prioritized and are linear in that some things need to be finished before other things can happen.

A good list is a tool every salesperson should use. No matter what format you prefer, a list can help you to remember and achieve things that are important to you. Starting your day without a list is like going to Omaha without a map—it is really hard to get there. Using lists properly is just another way to effectively manage your time. Like the Nike phrase says, "Just Do It." You'll get a lot more accomplished every day.

MAKING APPOINTMENTS

Unfaithfulness in the keeping of an appointment is an
act of clear dishonesty. You may as well borrow a person's
money as his time.
- Horace Mann

How many times have you heard "I can't see you without an appointment?" What a blow after you have been sitting in traffic for the better part of an hour You can then either plead, pout, or make an appointment. Usually the latter presents the best impression.

Cold calls are just those, cold calls. They do not have appointments set ahead of time. There is, of course, that obvious exception. But mostly, appointments are made with accounts that you have spent time with on a prior visit. You know when you leave that you have to make an appointment for future calls, so you plan accordingly and call prior to making that stop in the future.

Salespeople often ask me "Should I make appointments?" My answer is, it depends totally on the account. There is little that makes some accounts madder than to have a salesperson just "drop in." Let me caution you that if you do take this approach, make sure you have a professional opening statement for the account. Little sounds worse than a salesperson stumbling into an account and saying "I was just wandering around and in the neighborhood and thought I'd pop in to see what's happening." Uh!

I was working with a salesman one time making a call on an account whose store was at the top of some stairs on the second floor. This was a big guy and he tripped on the top step. He fell into the store unannounced and said "We were in the area and just wanted to drop in." The shop owner was so shocked that he let us make the call. Even though a bit unconventional, the approach, though not extremely eloquent, worked because the salesperson was thinking and making himself the butt of the joke.

If you take the time to make an appointment, the account will appreciate that you set an agenda for the call. A quick fax can make the difference between a successful call and one that doesn't go anywhere. This also forces you to plan for the call. Another side benefit is that you get to tell the account how much time you want to take. If you have requested too much time, your account will let you know. That is guaranteed.

Appointments usually work well for both the salesperson and the account. If you take the time to make them, take the time to prepare. The benefits are big and the impression that you leave with the account will not be haphazard, but professional.

DEALING WITH MATURE MARKETS

Nothing is a waste of time if you use the experience wisely.
- Auguste Rodin

I'll never forget being told by a salesperson who worked for me at one point that he was unable to grow his business because he was working in a mature marketplace. I remember looking at him and saying "baloney." He lasted not quite another two weeks. He had set in his mind that he was never going to be able to increase his sales because his market had matured and all his opportunities to grow had evaporated from his grasp.

If you're dealing with a mature market, what formula should you use to make your territory grow in the coming year? My first question to myself would be "Is the market really mature or am I not looking in the right places for growth opportunities?" It is easy to say every stone has been turned and all avenues have been explored. It is not so easy to continue exploring new avenues to growth by finding new customers.

Here are a couple of suggestions to help you move forward if you perceive your marketplace to be mature.

- Do research. Where haven't you looked for new business? Phone books, libraries, internet?
- Make a plan and write it down.
- Talk to existing customers about expanding your business.
- Get outside opinions and suggestions. A friend may have more insight than you think.

- Examine other uses for your products that your competition hasn't tried.
- Become incredibly familiar with your competition on both a local and national scale.
- Keep score. Measure yourself. You can't see progress unless it is on your paycheck or written down somewhere.

Calling a market mature may have some validity if you are working for the government and making a census report. But for salespeople, markets only become as mature as you allow them to be in your own mind.

It is wise to re-evaluate your territories regularly for lost or new opportunities. Your results may surprise you.

An Office At Home

He is happiest, be he king or peasant, who finds peace in his home.
- Goethe

I was asked not long ago if I used a home office. I said that I had done so for several months, but the distractions had gotten so bad I decided to find an office outside the home. I did not take a tax deduction on the home office, but I did make some mental notes you might enjoy having, since many of you do operate from an office in your home.

The IRS lets you write off a portion of your home if you use it for business on a daily basis and are having clients visit you there. My accountant told me that by claiming you have an in-home office, you send up one of the biggest IRS flags that will get you audited. I have claimed the deduction in the past, but always with the understanding that I may be staring an audit right in the face. Keep receipts and good records just in case.

One guy I know who works out of his home actually dresses in a coat and tie, eats breakfast, leaves the house, walks around the block, and returns to his office to start his day. For him, this is the only way he can really feel he is "at work." I remember I was lucky to even make it to the shower by noon when I was working out of the house. The other side of that equation was that I never really left the office. I would get up at 3am to answer e-mail or do some other work that I deemed necessary at the time.

If you work at home, here are a few tips.

- Stay out of the refrigerator. If you don't, you will grow instead of your business.
- Set time aside to take breaks. Just as in a regular office, you need to get the blood circulating. Move around and give yourself time to think about things. You will be twice as productive.
- When you leave for the day, don't go back in the office until morning. The perpetual office should only belong to all-night brokers who have nothing better to do.
- Try to keep outside distractions to a minimum. Of course, there is nothing you can do about barking dogs or crying children. But don't turn on the TV, and try to stay focused on the tasks at hand.
- Organize your work. Files, piles and lists. The better organized you are, the more productive you will have been at the end of the day.
- Don't just shuffle paper. Handle it once and be done with it. You will save yourself a huge amount of time.
- Return all phone calls during a set period of the day. This will help you avoid phone tag. Having a separate phone line for your business will help separate business calls from personal calls.

Having an office at home can be very beneficial if you use it correctly, but it can be equally harmful if it isn't utilized properly. The size of the office is not important, but the amount of productivity from the individual is. If you can be organized and productive working at home, a home office might be the right choice for you.

PEAKS & PLATEAUS

If the mountain won't come to Mohammed,
Mohammed must go to the mountain.
- English Proverb

I like to climb mountains. I enjoy the exhilaration of setting a goal to accomplish and then attaining it. Many have asked "What in the world makes you want to do this?" I can only explain that because the goal takes total concentration to attain, my mind rests from all the daily issues and distractions that occur. I become totally absorbed in the task at hand with my sole purpose to reach the summit.

Along the way, I encounter many peaks and plateaus that have to be scaled before I reach the top of the mountain. These steps are additional small accomplishments, which add up along the way to reaching the ultimate goal, which is the summit. If you really stop to think about it, we encounter the same thing in our day-to-day business lives. We have peaks and plateaus that have to be dealt with along the way, all hopefully leading to the ultimate goal for ourselves and our companies: success.

When I climb, I never climb without a partner. When I head out into the wide unknown to try to accomplish my goal, we always let someone know where we're going, when we're leaving and when we hope to return. That way, if we encounter some trouble along the way, somebody will start to wonder why we didn't return. Hopefully, they would also send some help to find my climbing partner and me. By planning ahead and taking precautions, we maximize our chances for success.

Another lesson hard-learned was: always take ropes. These ropes are your support system when you climb. If you need them and you haven't got them, you can be in big trouble. When you sell, you also need a support system to help you out of difficult situations. The support can come from a variety of areas, like your company, family, or peers. Check your support system regularly, just as you would if you were hanging from a rope.

To reach the summit in business you will need to climb a lot of peaks and walk some plateaus. Not always the easiest task, but the only way to accomplish your goals as a salesperson and as a company. If you give up, you will not make it to the summit. Many things go into making the task a success: strategy, good planning, preparation, proper equipment, your partner, and the ability to press onward when the summit comes into view.

Failing to reach the summit is a tragedy, because it means all the planning and preparation was for nothing. You didn't attain your goal when you were so close. Each of us have our own peaks and plateaus to deal with daily. Running a sales territory is no different from climbing a mountain. When you hit a difficult pitch, ask for help. When you need assistance, use your support staff. Don't give up. If you do, none of us will summit and we should all plan to do that together.

PHONE TIME

There is more to life than increasing its speed.
- Gandhi

How much of your time should be devoted to the phone? That depends on the circumstance and the salesperson. With today's communication expectations from the company you work for, and the customers you service, more time than ever is needed for the phone. Whether it is leaving a message on voice-mail or a personal conversation to set an appointment, phone time can be a valuable tool if used properly.

One of the greatest misperceptions that salespeople have is that a phone call can take the place of a personal visit. Nothing could be further from the truth. When was that last time you could fax a handshake or send a doughnut through the phone lines? It is that little something extra that your customers enjoy, having you in their place of business, learning how you and your products will help them make money. Because, after all, making money is why your customers are in business.

Phones are a great way to set appointments, check on quality issues, verify shipping, or even call the boss. But as a substitute for time spent with the customer, you are fooling yourself. Nothing makes a customer angrier than a salesperson calling with no apparent reason other than "just checking in."

- Always have a specific purpose for your phone call and state the reason at the outset so the customer can know why you are calling.
- Be concise. Nobody likes a phone call that drones on and on. Brevity should always be the order of the day.
- Listen. Nothing can be more frustrating than not being able to get a word in edgewise with an over talkative salesperson.
- Follow up. Do what you promise to do and do it quickly. If you wait for a couple of weeks to complete your follow-up, chances of the customer remembering your phone conversation are slim. Actions always speak louder than words.

Phones are a tool. They are no substitute for a live sales call. Use the tool wisely and not as your daily means of selling.

POST-CALL REVIEWS

People are always blaming their circumstances for what they are. I don't believe in circumstances. The people who get on in this world are the people who get up and look for the circumstances they want, and, if they can't find them, make them.
- George Bernard Shaw

One my favorite questions to ask a salesperson after we have completed a sales call is "What went right in that call?" It isn't a difficult question, but it makes you sit back and think about the call content. Usually, there are several good things that happened during the sales call. If not, you really blew the call. Good things can be anything from finding out the dog's name to writing a major order after a program presentation. These are things that should be written in the account's file or computer customer management system and will be helpful in dealing with the account in the future.

On the flip side, I also want to know what went wrong during the call. This again provides a self-evaluation tool for the salesperson, reflecting on techniques or topics which could have been steered in a positive direction, but went the wrong way. It is fun to be able to say things couldn't have gone better. But the reality is, things can always be better, and the self-evaluation process is a healthy tool to make sure the next call will be superior to the one just finished.

Finally, recognizing that some things may not have gone as planned, I ask what could have been done to improve the quality of the sales call. I have never had a salesperson say "nothing." It can be anything from providing better proofs or collateral materials to using better questioning techniques. Each sales call is different.

Missed opportunities need to be recognized and document-ed. If they aren't, you have become a PR person for your company and not a salesperson. Strive to make each call worthwhile and when it is completed, take that little bit of extra time for reflection. It will return to you a myriad of ideas and opportunities for future improvement in your sales techniques.

Practice Makes Perfect

Do what you love. Know your own bone; gnaw at it, bury it,
unearth it, and gnaw at it still.
- Henry David Thoreau

My son, Brad, started playing baseball a few years ago.
At his age, the technical name for it is T-Ball. For those of
you who don't know the difference between baseball and
T-ball, the batter gets to place the ball on a tie and hit it.
There is no pitching at this level. Brad was fortunate
enough to get on a team that had three coaches, one of
whom was the local high school baseball coach. Each kid
got a great deal of individual instruction in all aspects of
the game. I have to admit that the level of play was accel-
erated to the point where I was amazed to see 5 and 6-
year-old kids were actually able to turn a double play.

As most fathers, hoping for another Mark McGuire, I
worked with Brad regularly on his hitting, throwing and
catching techniques. I remember the surprise on his face
the first time he caught a pop fly—he didn't know how it
had ended up in his glove. (As a side note, the glove was
purchased when he was 2 weeks old and was kept in his
crib the entire duration of his infancy.) After he caught the
fly ball, I called "Hey, great catch." He smiled and said
"practice makes perfect." I became doubly proud because
not only had he caught the ball, he also had regurgitated
one of my favorite sayings. He had grasped the concept of
practicing for improvement. Not bad for a 5-year-old.

In virtually every aspect of business, some form of
practice is necessary for us to succeed. This is particularly
true in sales. A good salesperson can just show up and

sometimes will walk away with an order. But a great salesperson will practice everything regularly, from his one-on-one delivery to the most polished speech for a big group of people.

Recently, a CNN (Cable News Network) sports report was showing the Play of the Day. In this play, a college sophomore at the University of Wisconsin sank three half-court shots in a row and won two years of free college tuition. After making the third shot, a reporter asked him how often he practiced. He said that he hadn't touched a basketball in five years. Can you imagine how good this guy could be if he practiced? Being lucky is just that, lucky. Chances of him ever repeating the feat are a million to one.

Not many salespeople are perfect. Most of us have to work pretty hard to be successful. Practice is usually not very exciting. But when it counts, having taken the time to practice will improve your level of confidence, make your product knowledge grow, and increase your ability to present material better than you can imagine. You may not be able to recognize the difference, but trust me here, your client certainly will.

PROSPECTING

There's gold in them thar hills.
- Anonymous

Every time I hear the term "prospecting" it conjures up images of old westerns. These was always some old cowboy or miner in search of that pot of gold at the end of the rainbow, looking for that big gold strike that would make them rich. If you look up prospecting in the dictionary, you will see it defined as looking for something of worth. This definition certainly fits a sales definition as well. Prospecting is the act of looking for new clients who will deliver worth to you and your company.

Look in areas of potential worth when you prospect. When the old miners were out looking for a vein of gold, they always looked where someone else had found a big nugget. This is no different in sales. It is great to go off the beaten track to find new opportunities, and you should be encouraged to do just that on occasion. But most big prospective accounts are in our very own industry, yet to be found. I once had a salesperson tell me he knew everyone in the industry. I quickly pointed out that I seriously doubted this, because there are always new people coming into the business, and the industry was experiencing a constant changing flow of people at that time. When I mentioned a few names and asked if he knew them, he quickly realized that he really didn't know everyone in the industry. I assured him I didn't know everyone in the industry either.

The point is, each of us has our own set of contacts, our own industry network if you will. You most often hear about networking when people are looking for a new job. But using networks of people within your industry will help you to find prospects that might otherwise go unknown to you and your company. Networking is a learned skill. Being able to work within a variety of networks allows you to find those hidden nuggets that will produce gold for you in your business.   .

Sales forces are usually made up of a diverse group of people, each of whom has a network of their own. If you have the opportunity, take the time to investigate your co-worker's network for business. Your customers also work within their own networks. Take the time to explore these networks as much as possible. Ask questions about them. Many will turn up precious nuggets that can mean sales to you.

SALES CASE AUDITS

Next week there can't be any crisis. My schedule is already full.
- Henry A. Kissinger

When was the last time you checked to see if you had samples of all your products? Product lines today change quickly. Products are added, deleted, changed, or re-engineered. This happens periodically with all companies. If it doesn't the company is probably in a downward fall. This is particularly true in the design business. Never before have consumers been more in tune with design trends and colors, which results in companies introducing more products more quickly than ever before.

New product introductions can cause concern at the distribution level, since they are in the middle when the manufacturer introduces new things. They feel they have to pick up the new product to stay current. But as more and more product is introduced, a product saturation point will occur due to inventory and space requirements, which could eventually make the distributor audit not only the products, but also the vendor.

As salespeople, your samples are tools of the trade. The old adage "you can't sell it if you don't show it" holds true even today. Ways of presenting the samples are changing and evolving with the introduction of laptop computers into the sales call. But even here, periodic updates and information audits are necessary to make sure that you have all the products listed in your catalog available for your presentation.

A sample audit gives you time to review the line in thorough detail, refamiliarizing yourself with your favorites and re-introducing older products which may have been forgotten in the flurry of new products recently introduced. It also provides you with the opportunity to check your cases for missing product samples, either given away to a customer, or maybe never provided by the company in the first place. In either case, finding one missing product, however small it may be, will give you more to sell.

SELLING SLUMPS

*Opportunity is missed by most people because it is dressed
in overalls and looks like work.*
- Thomas A. Edison

It is not uncommon for salespeople to get into a selling slump at some point in their career. The salesperson doesn't recognize it at first, but the number of orders written declines, sales presentations become routine, the customers seem lethargic about new product introductions, and a variety of other telltale signs start to emerge. Wham! It hits you hard on Friday night after you get home from a four-hour drive that ended the week with nothing to show for it except extra miles on the car. You're having a sales slump. Things are not going well and you don't know why.

Here are a few ideas I would recommend if you feel you are either beginning a sales slump or are currently in the midst of one.

• Re-assess your plan. Are you on target to accomplish the goals you and your company have set for you? It is doubtful you are on plan. Check to see if the plan needs reworking and the goals are attainable. If they aren't, work with your sales manager to put a new plan in place with targets that can be reached. Nothing is more frustrating than attempting to achieve a goal that will never be attained, no matter how hard you work.

- Vary your routine and technique. Get up earlier, rework your weekly, monthly, or quarterly schedule. Every aspect of your time management should be scrutinized. Ask yourself: what is one thing you could stop doing, or start doing, or do differently starting today that would enhance the quality of your work? Then do it.

- Take some time off. When you are stale, there will be little you can do without taking some time off. I have had many salespeople tell me they have never worked harder and accomplished less. Maybe that is the problem. We cannot work hard all day every day and expect to be at the top of our game at all times. We are only human, and humans get tired physically and mentally. Take some time off to recharge your batteries. You will notice a big improvement quickly.

- Exercise regularly. Being fit is a big part of the equation. If you feel good, you are probably exercising at least three times a week. When we exercise, our bodies produce endorphins that give us more energy. You will be sharper every day if you exercise.

- Check your measurements. If you measure it, you will improve. Design your own critical measurements, ones that are not given to you by the company. Whether it is a weekly dollar sales target, or new customers gained, measure yourself. Nothing will make you feel better about yourself than seeing your own personal measurements improve.

These are just a few suggestions. Get input from your friends, family and customers. They are the ones who know you the best. Sales slumps aren't fatal, but they can drag us down quickly. They cause extra pressure from the boss and in most cases, a sales slump can put huge pressure on you in many facets of your life. Take time to analyze and deal with the issue professionally. The sooner your are out of the slump, the sooner life will seem good again.

TAKING NOTES

Long sentences in a short composition
are like large rooms in a little house.
- Shenstone

When I was in school, my teachers pounded into my head the importance of taking notes while I was in class. Today, now that I am in the business world, I have found that this important technique is no less important. I want to make sure I don't forget anything, and with the amount of information that flows my way these days, the only way to make sure that all the details are captured is to take a few notes now and then.

There are a few techniques that you should think about implementing if you do not currently think of yourself as a note-taker. First ask yourself: is this point noteworthy? If it contains a detail that needs to be recaptured at a later date, then you should write it down. You should be able to read your notes when you go back to look at them, as well as understand the important point you were trying to remember. The best test of note-taking is your ability to be able to read the contents at a later date.

Taking notes allows you to organize your ideas as well as those of the speaker. You are able to define an order in the speech content as well as set ideas down on paper or a computer—a process that could be the beginning of a solution to a problem you have been working on. Many people draw lines and symbols to help them organize their thoughts while listening.

It is always good to include a date in your notes. If, for some reason, you put the information in a place where you do not get to review it for some time, a date will help jog your memory about why you made the note.

Make your notes legible. Trying to put too much information on a single piece of paper can cause you a great deal of confusion. As a rule, always leave at least one inch of margin on the page to make sure you can decipher what has been placed on the paper. Key terms that are used should be noteworthy, including definitions that will have a special meaning later after the speaker has ended the presentation.

Labeling is another technique that many people use to recognize their note contents. Short phrases work well in this instance. Also key words and acronyms such as 'FYI' are important. When you have finished with a sales call, you should be able to revisit the account by simply looking at your notes. No one ever knows how important good notes are until they don't have them.

Weekend Warfare—
Swap Meets

Life is short. Live it up.
- Nikita Khrushchev

Nobody likes to work on weekends, particularly with the responsibilities of a family to attend to. But every now and then, the trade show planners require that we make an appearance at one of the industry trade shows that take place on the weekends. Some industries are worse than others about this, but the fact remains: if the company wants to participate, then somebody has to stand in the booth.

There are ways to get a little extra work done on the weekend and include the family. Many areas now have weekend art shows that cater to the family. Not only do you find wonderful pieces of art at great prices, there are also kiddy venues that include everything from snowcones to petting zoos. The atmosphere is very family-friendly and it is a great way to make contacts with potential customers.

One venue that is great for prospecting of new accounts is the swap meet. This venue has several different names around the country. If you are in the South, chances are you will be going to a flea market. In Texas, there is a venue called First Monday every month. In New England, you'll attend local county fairs, some indoors and others not. On the West Coast, it is the swap meet. All of them have many things offered because "one man's trash is another man's treasure." In recent years, these meets have become a great outlet for both retailers with store fronts and people who want to have or start a business without the hassles of a retail location.

Working weekends doesn't have to seem like work. Many family outings can have positive business effects without seeming like work. It can be great therapy as well as productive. So next time you are looking for a fun place to spend some time, consider some weekend warfare, and don't forget to take your business cards.

SELLING

GET TO THE DECISION-MAKER

Victory belongs to the most persevering.
- Napoleon

Talking to the right person on a sales call is critical. You can give your sales pitch, spend a great deal of time, go through an entire presentation, finish the call and then find out that your contact does not have the authority to make the buying decision. How can you prevent this enormous waste of time? Did you ask in the beginning who is the right person to deal with concerning buying issues? Did you spend all your time with one person when a joint buying decision needed to be made?

I once spent an entire day in a military complex being shuffled from one buying procurement office to another. I even asked if I needed additional input from other people at the base. All felt that a higher authority would need to make the final decision, but to "move the process along," I was advised to explain my company's program at each level, then move to the next in line in the procurement process. So I did. I knew they were interested in my products because they had called and requested I come to see them. Finally, at the end of the day, I walked into an office on the upper floor, occupied by a woman who asked me if it had been worth it. The whole day had been a process designed to discourage salespeople who gave up easily. The customer only wanted to work with salespeople who had the ability to get to the person who could make the decision. The government was at this time very unfriendly to vendors—they only wanted to work with companies that had the patience to persevere through the initial sales call. Since the salesperson represents that company, the stamina test had been put into place. Fortunately for me and my company, I made it through.

I'm not sure if I could make it through today. My patience level seems to be lower these days. But the fact remains; I did it then and got the government contract. It certainly would have been easier to have the decision-maker present at my first presentation. But knowing I was working through their process and would eventually get to the decision-maker helped me maintain my patience.

With distributor and OEM (original equipment manu-facturer) calls it is usually easier to quickly pinpoint the person making the decision. Retailers can present other challenges and are usually more difficult. Playing tag with an aloof owner who uses a front person as a barrier may require a bit more tact than when you immediately find the husband/wife owner team behind the counter. In the case of the aloof owner, the secretary or the person behind the counter can become your best friend. Treat them well— they are usually the people who can get you the audience you really need.

Getting to the decision-maker requires a few key elements:
1. Asking the right questions
2. Patience
3. Perseverance
4. Tact

Use all of these elements. Finding the person who can make decisions requires skill and maybe a little luck, but it must be done before the sale can be made.

DISCOUNTING & ALLOWANCES

It takes two to make a bargain.
- English Proverb

There is no substitute for a good discount; customers love them. But as salespeople in the field, you should be aware that a discount can be used as an effective selling tool to leverage your selling power with most retailers in the marketplace. What's a good discount worth? It is worth as much as you position it to be.

Discounts should not simply be viewed as a price concession. It is certainly that, and if you don't believe it, ask your immediate manager for additional discounts for a specific customer. You will always need reasonable justification for giving away margin in the form of an additional discount. A well thought-out justification will usually make getting approval much easier. Be ready to answer some of the following questions:

- What is the account's current revenue year-to-date, versus last year?
- What is the current discount, if any, of the account?
- What is the discount being proposed and what will be the impact on sales revenue?
- Is the discount temporary or permanent?
- In return for the discount, have other opportunities been explored with the account?

The last question highlights the fact that discounts can be used as effective tools in the selling process. Many salespeople give discounts freely, but fail to see them as opportunities to grow the account. Here are a few of the things you might ask from your account in return:

- Is the account willing to give you a specific percentage of their business purchases? Can this percentage be equated to dollars?
- Is the account willing to give up the discount if the requested dollars are not met?
- Are there other mainstream or peripheral products that can be placed in the account?
- Is the account willing to position your company as one of their top vendors?

Discounts today come in many forms. Here are just a few types of discounts offered to clients these days:
- Product, individual and combined
- Terms
- Freight
- Obsolete inventory (also known as buybacks)
- Advertising Allowances
- Merchandising Allowances
- Slotting Allowances
- Sampling
- Margin Allowances

My grandfather used to say, "What good is a big stick if you don't know how to use it?" Discounts and allowances should be considered "big sticks" in business. It never hurts to ask for something in return when you are providing your customer with a discount. You will be surprised at what you can gain from the account in return.

Featuring Older Products

A little experience often upsets a lot of theory.
- Cadman

Contrary to the popular belief of most salespeople, there is nothing wrong with re-introducing old products during a sales call. Everyone likes to show new things that are perceived as "new" or "cutting edge," but the truth of the matter is that old products, the basic day-in and day-out sellers, are the products that pay your salary.

When new products are shown for the first time, the customer often experiences "visual overload". Seldom does the customer glean all of the features and benefits of the new products during that first viewing. As a result, products are skipped over or passed up until the next visit—and by then the salesperson has new products to show; the new ones from the last showing are back in the sample case forgotten.

Customers usually know what they like or dislike. However, with the marketplace changing quickly in both trends and designs, many older products may fit new needs the customer is experiencing. This is a great reason to re-introduce or "feature" older products.

Another side benefit to featuring older products is that it allows the salesperson to become part of the marketing department. Who better to monitor and know the market than the field salesperson? Product selections that fit the individual market become a personal challenge, to keep the presentation fresh and walk away with the order. New collections that are account, market, or region specific can be put together from individual products of prior collections. All it takes is a little creativity and a healthy dose of knowing your accounts.

Remember, older products aren't bad products, they just aren't new. Challenge yourself to resell them from time to time. I think you will be surprised at how successful this can be.

FOLLOW THROUGH

He is an incorrigible ass who will never listen to others.
- Baltasar Gracián

Years of experience have taught me that nothing is more important in business than following through. Many salespeople realize this from the very beginning. If something falls through the cracks, they are the ones who usually get the blame. The customer is only interested in getting things done that were promised, either during the sales call or by the company. It is a critical time after the sale has been made, making sure those little details, some of which are large details, are taken care of quickly and with accuracy.

Customer service happens at many levels. It cannot be departmentalized in today's business environment. The details can concern information on inventory arrival, shipping that goes through the traffic department, credit or billing issues, or just something as simple as calling the customer to thank them for the order. The salesperson can write it on the order form, or send a quick handwritten note, but a call from the salesperson's superior tells the account that their business relationship is being watched over at higher levels. The goodwill generated here can be measured in new or additional business from the account.

Nothing can harm your reputation with an account more than making a promise to follow up on an issue and then leaving it undone. With most salespeople today, your little electronic organizer can prompt you to get the details done. Make sure you take the necessary notes so nothing is forgotten after you leave the account. Selling requires massive amounts of follow through. Both you and your accounts will suffer if follow through isn't handled well.

It may require a timeline to make sure things happen in the proper order, or maybe it will be handled with a simple, quick phone call. No matter how big or how small, quick, accurate, detail-tracking is required to be a sales professional today. Don't forget the details that keep your customers happy and buying more from you.

From Whence Your Customers Cometh

Sometimes when I consider what tremendous consequences come from little things...I am tempted to think...there are no little things.
- Bruce Barton

When we sit down and look at where our customers come from, inevitably they come from one place: leads. Most companies spend a great deal of money advertising their wares to get new prospects and current customers interested in their products. Prospects return the ad cards, then a list is collated from the cards. These leads are generally divided by territory and sent to the proper salesperson to do the follow-up. It has been my experience that many of these leads turn out to be a home or apartment one-person business. But then there is that one that makes these lists worth going through with a fine-toothed comb: the big kahuna, the major account buyer who likes what he sees but hasn't taken the time to contact the company directly. Now that's a lead!

Referrals are a great source for new leads. Financial planners, insurance agents and consultants thrive on this approach. They ask for leads at every call, and usually add: "If you think of someone later, just write the name down on the back of your business card and drop it in the mail to me." Not a bad approach, but not great if you are working retailers—most don't want to give you the names of their competitors. However, most do have friends in the business and they will offer those names freely during sales calls. It is a good idea to ask if they mind if you contact those people. Most will say "by all means," but a few are truly proprietary, not wanting to share information.

Leads today come in many forms. You may receive a computer diskette or just a plain paper copy of your listing. Phone books are a good source of leads, and so are libraries, web sites, conversations with competitors, conversations with customers—all can provide a good source for finding new prospects.

Where do your customers come from? They come from ferreting through that weekly maze of company mail, follow-up, and a great deal of hard work. Companies today are continually asking "what have you done for me today?" Lead follow-up is a very good way to make sure something is happening for the benefit of both the company and you, today as well as tomorrow.

HIDING BAD NEWS— DON'T DO IT

*You can want to do the right thing, and you can even want
to do it for the right reasons. But if you don't apply the right
principles, you can still hit the wall.*
- Stephen Covey, First Things First

I really dislike receiving bad news in business. When I
receive bad news, it means I will have to pass it on to
someone else, either to people who work for me or to people who are customers. Either way, it has to be acknowl-
edged and dealt with when received.

There are several ways to handle bad news. You can
deal with it. You can ignore it. You can act like an ostrich,
bury your head in the sand, and pretend that it just doesn't
exist. The latter is probably one of the most detrimental
approaches when it comes to business. Nothing makes me
madder than to find out, after the fact, that bad news has
been hidden, serving someone's rationalized idea that
"what you don't know won't hurt you." I find this particularly distasteful.

Hopefully in business you are dealing with adult personalities. Life produces certain situations that are classified as bad news. Some may be avoidable, but others are
beyond anyone's control. Taking a mature approach
should be the norm rather than the exception. Hiding bad
news only postpones the issue rather than dealing with it
up front. Bad news usually means you have a problem.
But with every problem, you have an opportunity to right
the situation and make a big impression on your customer.
If you hide it, the bad news becomes worse when it all
finally comes to light.

I once had a boss who taught me that honesty is always the best policy in business. Those little white lies come back to haunt you over time. If you have to pass on bad news, do it and don't hide it. Everyone involved will appreciate the way you handled the problem. Even though the news may not be good, dealing with it in a professional manner will increase your integrity and your value to the person you are dealing with at every level. Got bad news? Don't hide it. Deal with it and you will have better news tomorrow.

INCREASING SALES TO PRESENT CUSTOMERS

I don't have anything against work. I just figure, why deprive
somebody who really loves it?
- Dobie Gillis

Business schools teach their students a matrix that
shows them where all their potential business is expected
to come from. Two of the quadrants that are discussed in
detail concern sales to present customers. You can
increase sales to present customers through new product
introductions, or by increasing the amount of current products that are being shipped to the customer's account. Of
course, there are other means to increase sales, but the
inevitable result is getting more products shipped, billed,
and replaced in the customer chain.

New Products to Old Customers	Old Products to New Customers
Old Products to Old Customers	New Products to New Customers

The above matrix shows you the optimum way to grow
your business in your territory. Most sales approaches
start in the lower left-hand quadrant and form a bell-curve
that touches all four quadrants with the curve ending in the
lower right-hand quadrant. You do not always have both
new products and new customers, even though it would be
nice.

Most of us approach business in the lower left-hand quadrant first because it is the easiest. There is a comfort level that we have with old products and old customers. But there isn't as much challenge as selling to the other three quadrants. You have to prepare yourself in other ways to make sales in these areas happen.

Staple product lines, with systematic new product introductions that provide innovation, style, and sales growth drive business. Companies work hard to keep present customers focused on staple products as well as providing some new products. New product introductions should be frequent. But this should be only one focus of increasing sales to present customers. Don't forget about the other quadrants. Sales of the core product line must continue in order for the company to stay healthy. Sales of these products provide ongoing investment capital to support the new product introductions. Without these sales, the company will grow at a much slower pace than wanted.

For every dollar spent getting a new customer, five dollars are spent regaining one. As you're planning for growth in your territory, you should be involved in every quadrant listed above. But don't forget it is those present customers who will need the extra attention.

LAUNCHING NEW PRODUCTS

Only two things are infinite, the universe and human stupidity,
and I'm not sure about the former.
- Albert Einstein

The importance of launching new products cannot be underestimated in today's marketplace. It takes a great deal of effort internally before salespeople receive the benefits of being able to promote and show cutting edge introductions. These efforts include setting up vendor relationships, determining style and finish needs in relation to the current product line, development of internal monitoring for inventory needs and reordering, development of promotional materials, sales spiffs, pricing, sampling, target account assignments, and introductions into major chain account programs, just to name a few.

I wanted to bring these things to your attention because new product selections will be an important part of your growth. Your input is necessary to make sure all of the sales and marketing staff is up-to-date on your needs in the field. I encourage you to ask questions of your customers and get their input concerning trends, colors, and styles. Once you get this information, make sure this valuable information is written down and sent to the home office. The timeliness of the information should be considered critical.

Product launches can only be successful if the salespeople do their part. This should include complete familiarization with the new launch, a territory launch plan (where should you go first?), organization of all collateral materials, and practice of your new product presentation.

Opportunities don't usually just happen; most are created by hard work. Product launches are hard work but critical to the success of every company. You as salespeople are the vehicle that makes this success happen. Have fun with it and always remember the hard work that happened before the product hit your hands. Don't miss the opportunity to make every new product launch a personal and company success.

Pre-call Planning

When love and skill work together, expect a masterpiece.
- John Ruskin

When I have traveled with salespeople in the past, it is incredibly evident which ones have a pre-call planning process versus those who don't. When you have taken time to think about what you want to accomplish during the sales call, the chances of walking out with an order increase at least 100-fold. Of course, there will always be "Mr. Lucky" who never plans and somehow stumbles out with an order. But for most of us, the pre-call planning process is very helpful and significantly impacts every part of the sales call.

What does pre-call planning consist of? It is a chance to reacquaint yourself with the account. This includes constructing a specific set of written objectives for each call. The objectives can be as small as updating the account's catalog, or as grandiose as a full-blown presentation for the entire Board of Directors. Regardless, you should write down all your objectives before you walk through the door and refer to them as necessary during the call to make sure you cover all the topics.

Have pertinent sales data and records ready for the account if necessary. This includes a sales history and specific sales targets for current and past years. Many salespeople are now automated and this information can be easily downloaded from the home office. For those who aren't, request this information at least a week before you need it. That gives everyone involved in the information-gathering process time to prepare the reports prior to your call.

Make sure your opening statement is well polished and states the reason(s) for your call, the amount of time you will need, and what you would like to discuss during the meeting. Also, make sure you have at least five good open-ended questions which you have practiced and specially tailored for the account call.

Most professional salespeople have a specific opening statement they can recite in their sleep. Daily practice of the presentation makes it more professional, until your opening statement is so fluid the words become a natural part of the opening conversation. If you haven't taken the time to learn or formulate your opening statement, I encourage you to do so.

Prepare any proofs and presentation materials you need to bring with you during your presentation. Nothing makes a salesperson look more unprofessional than fumbling in a briefcase or having to return to the car during a meeting.

Lastly, review any opportunities you uncovered from your last call which could present a sale opportunity for you. It is always a good idea to review the personal information you have gathered so you remember the names of the wife, kids, and even the family pet. This will count for major points as your personal relationship grows with the account over the years.

Pre-call planning is one of the most overlooked parts of the sales call. Make sure you are prepared when your manager decides to ride with you. Your job may depend upon it.

PROBING FOR NEEDS

A man would do well to carry a pencil in his pocket, and write down the thoughts of the moment. Those that come unsought for are commonly the most valuable, and should be secured, because they seldom return.
- Francis Bacon

A need is an opportunity to make a sale. It can be presented to you unsolicited; however, most salespeople have to dig to find a need. Finding a need is an opportunity to solve a problem for your customer or prospect. It ingratiates you and allows you to move forward to provide superior service to them. In most cases, needs are not just presented to salespeople, they have to be pulled out of the customer. This is an acquired skill that takes practice.

Your questioning technique is paramount. Always start by asking an open-ended question. These are questions that cannot be answered with a simple yes or no. Some examples of open-ended questions are:

Tell me about your business.
What brought you to this business?
What are your criteria for making a decision?
What are your expectations of a supplier?

Don't ask...
What's happening today?
Is price an important factor to you?
How quickly do you need the product?
Can I call on the guy down the street?

It is tough to explore needs when the conversation turns to the local sports team unless you are selling sporting goods. Ask questions about topics that are important to your customer. Stay focused and you will have a better opportunity to discover a need.

When you find those hot buttons, begin to narrow your focus toward the close. Compress the topic by asking more and more defined questions that eventually lead you to the sale.

If you remember these three things, you will be on your way to extracting your customer's needs.

1. Begin with open-ended questions.
2. Focus on issues that matter.
3. Narrow your focus toward the close.

RECOGNIZING BUYING SIGNALS

To climb steep hills requires a slow pace at first.
- William Shakespeare, Henry VII, Act 1, Scene 1

When was the last time you had a customer or prospect sit back, raise their hand, and say, "I'm ready to buy?" Probably not lately. So how does a salesperson know when to go for the close? By recognizing buying signals and being patient. Both are a learned art, but both are incredibly important to your success in the field.

Buying signals come in a variety of forms. It can be as little as a raised eyebrow during your presentation, or the ultimate buying signal—when the customer says, "Let's write the order." The real key to recognizing these signals is to be observant and be a good listener.

Body language can tell you a great deal. It can tell the salesperson quickly how the prospect is feeling about what is being said. It can say "Tell me more" or it can say "Shut-up and go away." If you feel the latter is happening, it is time to ask more questions because you are not addressing a specific need. Find that need and watch the body language change from disengaged to interested very quickly.

Watch for crossed arms, unaccepting facial expressions, hands on the hips, a turned back; these can signal that the prospect has lost interest. On the other side, watch for raised eyebrows or other inquiring facial looks, a nodding head saying "yes" as opposed to "no," an introduction to a co-worker who has input; all can be signs that the prospect has an interest in what you are saying.

Questions about your products or company can be a buying signal. If there was no interest, they would not be curious about whom you work for, the company policies, or shipping locations. If you listen to their questions, these can be excellent buying signals.

Watch for explanations about the prospect's business and comments about specific opportunities for problem-solving. If you can solve a prospective need, the opportunity for the next step becomes much easier. Presentation of a need or problem can be a buying signal.

You, as a salesperson, have to be patient and wait for buying signals. But just as important as waiting for them is recognizing them when they happen. When they do, go for the close. Choosing the moment for this is an individual decision, but when buying signals are presented, it is important to take advantage of the opening.

WHAT'S A RUMOR WORTH?

There is only one thing in the world worse than being talked about,
and that is not being talked about.
- Oscar Wilde, The Picture of Dorian Gray

I got a phone call from a sales rep not too long ago who was being talked about by another competitive salesperson. He was suggesting, and I use this term loosely, that the other salesperson was leaving his company in search of greener pastures. This upset the gentleman who called me because there was absolutely no truth to the rumor. He wanted to know how he should handle this circumstance.

Rumors are a quick way to get a rise out of your customer. You feel like you are passing on important information to the customer, when in fact you are damaging your reputation as a professional. Facts are what business is all about. I have yet to see a successful business owner who functioned solely on industry rumors or who profited from them. Rumors can be malicious or frivolous, but whatever the form, a rumor is still a rumor.

Being a "rumormonger" shows a complete lack of professionalism. When a juicy rumor surfaces in the industry, everyone wants to be the first to pass it on to the unknowing at the next level. I have yet to see a professional salesperson have "spreading a rumor" on his or her pre-call planning list. Information-gathering may include hearing a rumor from your customer, but it should not be part of your sales pitch at any time.

It seems to be a natural occurrence that rumors take on a life of their own with no concern for who might be hurt in the process. Small untruths are embellished until they become further and further from the original untruth. They have no regard for who or what may be run over in their path. I was once in a seminar of about 20 people where the group played a game. The leader had us line up and whispered something in the first person's ear. We were to listen and pass on what was said to the next person. By the time the original phrase reached the end of the line, it was completely different from what the leader had originally whispered to the first person.

This was a listening exercise. But I believe it also appropriately illustrates how a rumor can quickly and easily be embellished, gather momentum, and take on a new life every time it is repeated in the marketplace. Being in field sales does not sanction us to repeat things from one account to the next. I have not met an account yet that likes to be talked about to their competition down the road. I also believe that salespeople who spread rumors are less likely to get the account to trust them, which will cost them a great deal of present and future sales.

My comment to the gentleman that called me for advice: at least they are talking about you. Rise above it and use your professionalism to counter the rumor and the competitive salesman who was spreading it. It will help you in the long run and hurt your competition where it counts the most, in your customer's eyes. Stay away from the rumor mill. It is not in your job description.

SELLING LIKE A TURKEY

Toleration is the best religion.
- Victor Hugo

Thanksgiving has traditionally been a very bad day for turkeys. Although they are considered the dumbest bird in the animal kingdom, I feel sure there are lessons we can learn from these delicious-tasting birds.

Turkeys got their reputation for being stupid a long time ago. When it rains, the turkey looks up to see where the rain is coming from. Sometimes it doesn't stop looking until the bird has drowned itself. Farmers learned this and now all turkey farms have covered houses to keep the birds out of the rain.

The turkey was also the first gift the Pilgrims received from the local Native Americans in Jamestown. The locals thought to themselves, "Check out these guys. They deserve an award for attempting to stay through the winter. What a bunch of turkeys. Let's give them one." And the American tradition of sharing a turkey dinner was born.

Whatever the shortcomings or virtues of these birds, noone wants to be a turkey. Be careful, because being in sales can afford you many opportunities to be one. Going into the account unprepared, not knowing your product line or company policies, passing responsibility for taking care of issues to someone else, presenting a poor image, talking badly about your competition, asking uninformed questions—these are just a few ways to make yourself look like a turkey when you make a sales call.

So next time you head into a call, make sure your wattle isn't showing and the first thing out of your mouth isn't "gobble, gobble." Sell like the professional you are, not like a turkey. Have a great Thanksgiving. I'm thankful for all of you who are sales professionals.

Spur of the Moment Policy

Anger makes dull men witty, but it keeps them poor.
- Francis Bacon

We have to deal with company policy every day. Policies and procedures are very necessary to make a company function. Policy prevents employees from making snap judgements in situations that effect the company in every aspect from profit margins to sales discounts. Having set policies and procedures in place allows you in sales to have distinct lines of demarcation by which you can measure your sales presentation to your customers.

You can usually find some of the important policies in your terms of sale. They will deal with credits and returns, product discount structures, shipping methods, etc. The company may choose to have separate and distinct policies on some issues that arise, such as a return goods policy, to make sure every part of the process is documented and followed.

Not long ago, I was traveling with a sales rep in the field doing an evaluation for a company. The salesperson had a few guidelines concerning company policy, but most of it was very unstructured. I asked him how he handled certain situations and he told me he would just call the sales manager, who would make a decision on the spot. The salesman was comfortable with this approach, but I doubted if the owner of the company would be if he knew how policy was being handed out, on the spur of the moment.

As a salesperson, you should never get yourself into a position where you are formulating company policy as the need arises. The issue should be documented and submitted to your managers; let them make the policy that is appropriate. You may be asked for your opinion, which you should give openly, but never think that a quick decision on your part without input from your boss will be in your best interest. It can not only be detrimental to you, but it could also be very costly to the company. If your boss chooses to enact spur of the moment policy, then you can run with it. But chances are good that most policy will be well thought out before it is formally put into place.

Most situations in the field have a way of repeating themselves at some point. That is why it is good to have a set policy to deal with the situation or issue. Don't invent spur of the moment policy in the field. Discuss issues with your company first and let the policy decision come from the home office. It may not be the answer you want, but it will prove to be the right approach for both you and your customer in the long run.

TAKING ANOTHER ROUTE

We can judge our progress by the courage of our questions and depth of our answers, our willingness to embrace what is true rather than what feels good.
- Carl Sagan

It is not uncommon for me to be accused of operating on the back roads. I have always enjoyed taking the scenic way to a destination, even if it took a little longer. I was always taught that the shortest distance between two points is a straight line. That is certainly true in math, but sometimes you need to take a different route in a sales call to produce the desired results. Even though the quickest way may be point to point, the customer may blow this lineal approach right out the window. You will have to resort to taking another route.

Consider the various possible strategies when redirecting your approach. Whenever prospective salespeople are interviewed, this subject is always addressed. How do you want to get where you want to go? If that doesn't work, what is your contingency plan? Are you able to get to the same end by taking different approaches? Give me some examples of this. By the end of the conversation, you can usually tell if the prospective salesperson can take different routes to achieve the same goals.

Professional salespeople have to be able to think on their feet. In every case, the customer is your variable. They may stop you during a presentation, ask an unexpected question, change conversation topics altogether, or simply say no at the end of the call. Being able to back up to a critical point, rephrase, and take another route to the close of the sale separates the good salesperson from the great salesperson.

Here are some tips to help you take another route if necessary.

1. As you plan for the sales call, identify the critical points of the call.
2. Experiment with phrasing, saying the same thing in different ways.
3. Let the words you use be your road map to the close.
4. Use your favorite alternate route to get to the next step when you have to back up during a call.

Mapping yourself multiple routes allows you multiple opportunities to have closure at the end of your call. I encourage you to operate on the back roads because the most creative ways to get there can be the most fun as well as the most successful.

THE WRITTEN WORD

*Noise proves nothing. Often a hen who has merely laid an egg
cackles as if she laid an asteroid.*
- Samuel Clemens

We are visual society. Businesses today must have a
visible reference which can be consulted as decisions are
made. As sales trainers, sales managers continually pound
the idea of listening into the heads of their people. But listening is only half the battle, because it allows you to recognize needs. But then the opportunities have to be sum-
marized for future reference. The needs and recommenda-
tions have to be written down somewhere. It is the written
word I am referring to in this instance. Tell me, but also
write it down so we can look at it, plan, and hopefully get
an action associated with the plan. If all goes well, that
means a sale to you.

There are numerous books written on the subject of
writing business proposals. In this instance, I'm not talking about a business plan that is the beginning of a business, but a business proposal that you as a salesperson are
developing for your client. The proposal will address the
current situation, the need that is currently being explored,
a proposed solution, and costs associated with the proposal. Sales professionals today are writing these types of
proposals regularly to expand their opportunities with both
current and potential clients.

These days, letters are not a luxury, they are a necessi-
ty. When was the last time you recalled a conversation or
a point about a prior meeting and the client remembered
the conversation in a totally different context? It can hap-

pen to anyone, but the best way to anticipate and guard against it is to have some sort of written word. This can be in the form of a letter, fax, or e-mail. The form is not important. It is a reference tool in your possession, not to correct the account, but to keep your call and conversation on the right track as the sale becomes closer to reality. There will be no questions about the terms and conditions if you take the time to restate your conversation in writing.

Companies can drown in their own bureaucratic methods—copying, recopying, sending and re-sending information from one department to another. It is the manager's responsibility to act on the written communication that crosses his or her desk. My policy has always been that if someone thought enough of a situation or idea to write it down, then it was worth reading. The same can be said for your clients; they will read your communication if it is written down. It brings them to your world on your terms without your presentation being interrupted or cut short.

Write it down. People will take the time to read what you have to say.

The Unspoken Word

*If your parents didn't have any children, there is
a good chance you won't have any.*
- Clarence Day

What makes you different from the next salesperson
that walks through your customer's door? Do you take the
time to deliver something a little extra, something that
doesn't require you to be in front of your customer? I
have found that many times a lasting impression is made
by small acts that I call the "unspoken word."

One common occurrence that has happened to all of us
in sales is arriving at an account with an appointment, and
finding the customer has had to leave for some reason.
The door is locked, and you are mad because your time
has been wasted. Many salespeople will just leave, hoping
to return later. But a more effective approach would be to
write a small note on the back of your business card and
leave it under the door. Even if you do not wish to return
later, you will leave a good impression with your
account—it is proof that you arrived on time as scheduled,
and are interested in rescheduling. The note will make a
lasting impression.

The same can be said about written follow-up cards or
thank you notes. It doesn't take much time or effort to
quickly write a short thank you for an order. Hand written
is always the best. Make sure your handwriting is legible
and not a frustration to read, or you might get the opposite
result of what you intended.

Letters are usually more formal and take more time.
You can always incorporate a thank you, but the main

intent is to reinforce events or issues that were discussed during your conversation with your customer. Brevity and good grammar will be accepted better than long flowing prose with many misspelled words.

One of my favorite tricks is to insert a business card in a visitor's coat pocket. I have to be a bit sneaky to get this done, but if I get caught, it is very explainable. They usually find these at some point in the future and have a very good reaction to this small unspoken word. Use your imagination to provide small acts that may make a big difference. It will provide you with many more opportunities to increase your sales, and will build a stronger relationship with your account.

DEALING
WITH
CUSTOMERS

ASKING THE RIGHT QUESTIONS, TO THE RIGHT PEOPLE

The best part of our knowledge is that which teaches us
where knowledge leaves off and ignorance begins.
- Oliver Wendell Holmes

Have you ever noticed how easy it is to get an answer to your question? I certainly have with every company I have ever worked for. The answer may not be the right one, or the one that I want to hear, but at least it is an answer I can take back to the customer. Or is it?

There are two parts to this issue. 1) Have I asked the right question? and if so, 2) have I directed the right question to the right person? If you have asked the wrong person, they will probably give you an answer, but chances are very good that it will not be the correct answer. Most salespeople just want an answer, regardless if it is right or wrong. Then, once the customer has been told the inappropriate answer, the responsibility of the wrong answer passes from the salesperson to the corporate office, which usually entails a great deal of finger pointing.

Developing the right line of communication is ultimately as important as getting the order. If you give the customer the wrong answers, it will cost you orders in the near and long term. Just getting an answer without knowing that you have asked the correct person, with the proper knowledge to give you the correct answer, doesn't always help your cause. Your cause and your customer's cause will be moved forward only by providing the customer with information that is timely, concise, and correct.

Assumptions are another issue that occur not only from asking the wrong question, but possibly from not asking the question at all. To assume is to guarantee yourself problems, both internally at the company and externally with your customers. Don't ever assume under any circumstances.

To cover yourself, make a list of areas where you consistently run into questions that need answers. You should have one company contact for each of these areas. If possible, you should always direct the question to your immediate supervisor or the departmental head. Once you have developed your list of questionable areas, go to the same person repeatedly to get the most reliable answers. If you don't know who that person is, ask. The only dumb question is the one that is not asked.

Try to speak directly to the person you believe will know the answer. Asking the right question to someone who may go to the wrong person for an answer doesn't do you any good. You will still get an answer, but not necessarily the right answer. You can't even be assured that your original question will be phrased in a way that will give you the correct answer you need.

Flow charts can help companies communicate on a professional level and, hopefully, you will not get multiple answers to the same questions.   Work hard to be consistent with your inside contacts. It is in everybody's best interest.

BEING IN FRONT OF THE CUSTOMER

A vacant mind invites dangerous inmates
- Nicholas Hilliard

Phone calls work sometimes. Faxes and letters work sometimes. But there is no substitute for being in front of your customer. Some salespeople actually get orders just for showing up. I once worked for a sales manager that told me "If you just make the calls, your territory will grow." While that is true to some extent, I now know there are a few more factors that play into the territory growth equation.

Being in front of the customer is a major part of the equation. I once worked for a company that had a big part of their business dealings in the international market. The company had hired international sales agents to work for them over a period of years. One gentleman that worked in the Asian market took me around to introduce me to his customers. After we came out of one call, he told me "Remember, you can never fax a handshake."

I have never forgotten that statement. That is what being in front of the customer is all about. Being able to see your customer's expression when they answer your questions, see what your competition is doing in the account, get a general idea of the flow of your customer's business—all these things require you to be in front of your customer.

As I stated earlier, just showing up isn't enough these days. The customer expects a professional appearance, presentation, and accurate answers to their questions. All of these require preparation on the salesperson's part. Your professionalism grows in the eyes of your client the more you prepare. You can tell the difference and your customer can tell the difference.

If you make the effort to be in front of your customer, being prepared can make or break the call. So when you do show up, be the best in all aspects. Your company is counting on you.

Profiling Customers

For knowledge, too, is itself a power.
- Sir Francis Bacon

All customers have certain characteristics that make them unique. The key to understanding how to play this card is remembering which customer has which unique feature. The feature can be something about their appearance, their family, their product selection, your competition, their financial situation, or even their parents if the characteristic is unique enough.

Customer profiling is a good way to capture information that best makes an account stand out or makes it different from your other accounts. Many years ago when I started traveling on the road, I would take red files and build a small information base about my most important customers. What made them important to me at that time was sales revenue because I was a commission salesman. If I didn't sell, I didn't eat. Building information about my most important accounts allowed me to focus on the most important aspects of their account, and also their most unique characteristics.

Today, with all the new electronic notebooks that are available, many salespeople use a customer profiling system built-in as part of their address book. The ability to keep notes is also usually part of the address book. This small feature allows you to customize and format a profile sheet that can include as much or as little data as you feel is necessary to keep concerning the account or prospect.

Profiling does not necessarily need to be limited to your current set of customers. It is also an excellent way to capture information on prospective clients that have not bought anything from you yet. In either case, finding those unique characteristics about the account and capturing the information is essential to helping you move forward with your sales plan for the account.

What should a customer profile include? It is really up to the person that is doing the profiling. But here are a few of my suggestions that you may find helpful.

- Financial information including sales history and credit information.
- Product selections and pertinent sales data.
- Competitive information.
- Programs that are of interest to the customers.
- All relative billing and shipping information.
- Family information.
- Important dates such as birthdays and anniversaries.
- Hobbies and other personal interests.

Should every account have a customer profile? In a perfect world, we would sell every product to every customer we have. But as you probably already know, this isn't the case. The customers that you feel are your top accounts currently, and those that have the potential to be a top account, should have a customer profile developed for them. Customer profiling is another tool that, if used wisely with information kept up to date, can become one of your biggest assets in the field. You have nothing to lose—except maybe sales lost from not using it.

DEALING WITH NEGATIVITY

Minds are like parachutes—they only function when open.
- Thomas Dewar

Nobody likes a negative person, particularly if you are a salesperson. But in some cases, negativity can be good. It can provide you with opportunities that would not otherwise be presented to you. Here are a few ways to turn a negative into a positive.

- Examine your approach. Did you do something to turn the account or situation into a negative situation? Re-examine your style, your content and your approach to this customer. It might make a big difference.
- Evaluate your current available programs. Maybe the guy who is so negative on the other side of the counter has some valid input about your current program offerings. Take notes and follow-up with the account to let them know their input was noted and worthwhile.
- Refine your answers to specific objections you encounter. If the person you are calling on is totally negative, why not turn the call into a practice session for the next sour SOB that you encounter. Overcoming objections is a learned skill which takes a great deal of practice.
- Solve the problem. People can become negative because they have run into a problem. Find the problem and get involved. You have the opportunity to make lemonade out of lemons.

- Don't let your own attitude become negative. Just because you have to deal with a sour individual, don't let them pull you into the quagmire. Rise above it and keep the call positive at all costs.

In the final analysis, there may not be anything you can do to turn the negative into a positive. But when all else fails, make sure you keep that positive attitude. Wear a smile and just maybe the smile will be returned.

DISARMING CUSTOMERS

*When I'm getting ready to reason with a man, I spend one-third of my time
thinking about myself and what I am going to say—and two-thirds
thinking about him and what he is going to say.*
- Abraham Lincoln

Every salesperson develops their own style over a period of time. The way you interact with current and prospective clients is a big part of your style. Salespeople need to provide a level of comfort for the accounts. This has to happen whether it is the first time or the fortieth time you meet with them. Your style provides you with ways to disarm your customers.

Tasteful humor is a very good way to put your customer at ease. Laughter always makes people loosen up. I have seen accounts become so loose that the entire integrity of the sales call goes out the window. The salesperson is not able to bring the call back into focus because they get off track telling jokes and stories. This is an extraordinary way to build rapport, but make sure you keep the humor clean and if possible, relate the material to your sales presentation.

Some customers like to keep the salesperson around for company. This can be difficult when you have other appointments during the day. In a case such as this, a surprise attack is a good way to move the call along to the next level. Ask a very pointed closed-ended question such as "are you ready to buy yet?" This will generally unclog the call and start to move things along. You should make sure you know the account well enough to try this approach. If not handled correctly, you may succeed in making your client or prospect angry.

Another gutsy approach is to have the customer rate your company. This provides you with ammunition to overcome objections prior to them being presented through questioning. If you take this approach, make sure you know that your account has been reasonably happy with your company. Low ratings will cause the account to think twice about the current business relationships with most of their vendors.

There is no substitute for using good judgement. There is a real art to disarming customers to the point where they are comfortable, and a mutual trust and respect has been established. One push in the wrong direction can produce the exact opposite effect that you are hoping to achieve. Be aware of the customer's immediate business environment. If they are having a bad day, be careful not to pour gasoline on an already raging fire.

Remember these pointers for disarming your customer:
1. Tasteful humor
2. Surprise attacks: "Are you ready to buy yet?"
3. Have the buyer rate your company
4. Use good judgement

Develop your own techniques for disarming your customers. It helps move the call count along as well as making each call much more enjoyable for both you and your customer.

EDUCATING YOUR CUSTOMER & YOURSELF

*Knowledge and human power are synonymous,
since the ignorance of the cause frustrates the effect.*
- Francis Bacon

Being a salesperson often includes being a teacher, particularly in the framing business. Picture framers look to their regular salespeople for ideas, information, and sometimes techniques that are being used by other people in the business. It can be difficult to draw the line between salesperson and teacher, but every great salesperson I have ever known has both qualities and is able to maneuver between both roles comfortably.

Don't be afraid to say "I don't know," but never fail to follow that with "But I'll find out." You have multiple resources available to you for finding answers.

Read your industry periodicals regularly. Many of your customers are contributing writers to these magazines. Not only does it provide you with information on the topic, it also allows you the opportunity to comment when you visit the writer. There are more articles than ever before available on specific topics and techniques. And nobody is saying that you have to be well-versed in every subject, but being able to speak intelligently on types of equipment, hardware, ancillary products, and specifically moulding variations and finishes is critical. A true professional is well-informed and is able to communicate valuable information to customers and associates.

Turn your car into an instrument of instruction. Audiotapes and CD's are available on a number of topics today. There is no better time to learn than when you're alone in the privacy of your own car. Take the time to practice out loud the topics you feel will be worthwhile in your next call.

Let's not forget the Internet as a source for gathering information. Many of the industry web sites have information that can be gleaned and regurgitated during a sales call. The opportunity to learn and then teach your customers is really only limited by your willingness to do so.

Your primary responsibility is to make the sales calls and write orders. But if you have the opportunity to provide some helpful information along the way, I encourage you to seize the moment.

CUSTOMER EYE CONTACT

He was a wise man who said: As I grow older I pay less attention to what men say. I just watch what they do.
- Wilfred A. Peterson

Nothing drives me crazier than talking to a person who won't look me in the eyes. It usually signals one of three things to me:

1. This person is lying to me.
2. This person has no interest in the present conversation.
3 This person doesn't know all the facts about the topic of conversation.

When I was a kid, my father always made me look him in the eye when I was giving him the answer to one of his questions. He always said, "You can tell if a person is really sincere when they look you in the eye." To this day, I still believe that and try to practice this regularly.

I have worked with many salespeople over the years. I was astounded to see that some of the very best lose eye contact with the buyer at the most critical part of the sale. It is difficult to get to the close if you lose eye contact, because it gives an impression that "this guy doesn't really care what I have to say." True or not, your customer may perceive glancing away as disinterest. It conveys an "I don't care" attitude that doesn't make the customer feel appreciated.

You can usually tell if a person is lying or is being insincere. Eyes drop or look away just as they make a statement. Kids are particularly good at this. You can always catch them when you make them look you in the eye. Adults are a little more difficult to read because you can't always tell them to look you in the eye during a business conversation.

Have you ever been standing in the aisle at a trade show and the person you are talking to keeps glancing over your shoulder or looking away? It always makes me feel like they are looking for someone more important to speak with, instead of focusing on the person with whom they are presently engaged in conversation. I always want to say "Do you mind looking this way until we have finished our conversation?" But I never do.

Losing eye contact can also mean the speaker does not know all the facts about the topic of conversation. Not much makes me lose attention faster than thinking I'm speaking with an uninformed person.

Salespeople have to be very cognizant of maintaining eye contact when they are with an account. When working with some salespeople, I watch them try to look at sample boards while making their presentation, or look at the shop surroundings so they can compliment the shop owner. This usually means the salesperson hasn't planned what to say before entering the store. It makes me uncomfortable to be a part of the call because the shop owner will turn to the other person, me, once the eye contact has been broken with the salesperson. I actually had one shop owner tell one salesman I was working with "Hey, I'm over here." And the guy still didn't get it. He did after we left the call.

Check yourself to make sure you are maintaining eye contact with the people you are talking to, whether at home or at work. It will not only make you seem interested, but you will improve your listening skills as well.

FIRST IMPRESSIONS

Well begun is half done.
- Horace

Every sales book I have ever read has a section on making a good first impression, so I guess I should include one as well. A first impression is something you only get one chance at. Once spent, you cannot get it back or start over again.

When I was a younger man working a territory day in and day out, I worked very hard to create a good first impression. I was 21 and hungry, working in Texas in the incredible heat of the summer. I always wore a coat and tie. I didn't care if it was 110 degrees in the shade; I was determined to leave a good first impression. After I had been in the territory for a few years, I eventually dropped the coat. Many of my customers started asking where my coat was. Usually I took it with me, but I would leave it in the car. If the customer asked, I would excuse myself, get the coat from my car and put it on. It became a small trademark of my selling style. I still run into old customers from time to time and they always bring up my wearing that coat and tie in the searing heat. Today, I realize they thought I was nuts, but still appreciated the effort I put forth.

On another occasion, I had gotten up for a very early appointment to show my products. I made it to the appointment on time and asked if I could show a few new products. As I bent over to reach in the sample case, my pants split from zipper to belt loop. I literally was wearing two pieces of cloth held together by my belt. You should have seen the expression on my prospect's face, not to mention the expression on my face. Fortunately, I was wearing a coat, which I immediately took off, tied around my waist and finished the call. Both of us laughed pretty hard about this the last time we saw one another because it was a first impression that was hard to beat and one I don't recommend making.

First impressions are created in a variety of ways. People remember how you are dressed, what your opening remarks are, how much cologne you wear, how well your fingernails are manicured. You have the ability, not to decide for the person meeting you for the first time, but certainly to influence their first impression of you. Make it a good one because you will never have the chance again.

GIVING ADVICE

Ninety percent of all human wisdom is the
ability to mind your own business.
- Robert A. Heinlein

As I was preparing a newsletter a few weeks ago, I came upon a short piece of advice that I found funny, yet very serious. Don't take Viagra before surgery. Now, I want to meet that man! As I sat here pondering the advice that was given, I thought maybe if I knew I was going into surgery, wanted a little special attention the night before and decided to pop a Viagra for good measure, I doubt I would think about the consequences of taking it before surgery. So, the advice would be valid.

I was relaying this story to another friend. He laughed and said he could see how the advice could be legitimate. But he would have been more inclined to tell the guy having surgery to mark the part that was being operated on, so no mistakes would be made. That is valid advice as well.

When customers ask for an opinion, I always try to give them a couple of options on each topic. That way, I'm not making the decision for them nor am I sounding like I have all the answers. There are pitfalls in giving advice to clients. If you give bad advice and the client takes it, you are the goat, not them. A good example of giving this type of advice comes from attorneys. There is an old saying, "You can lead a horse to water but you can't make him drink." If your advice makes a decision for the customer, you are forcing him to drink. That's not good.

On the other hand, advice when asked for is usually appreciated. Many companies pay people to get advice.

These people are called consultants. Today, that is exactly what many salespeople are becoming: consultants. They practice "consultative selling," offering advice on products, service, problem-solving, and other important issues that concern the salesperson's company and the client.

If you give advice, make sure it is appropriate to the business at hand. Stay away from issues that involve family, friends, employees, health, religion and politics. Advice can be your best friend or your worst enemy. In conclusion, let me say, do not take Viagra within 24 hours of surgery—and remind your surgeon what part to work on.

THE ACCOUNT THAT
WON'T LET YOU LEAVE

A fanatic is one who can't change his mind
and won't change the subject.
- Winston S. Churchill

Many of us have customers who love to talk. I have found that generally this type of customer falls into three categories: 1) lonesome, 2) know-it-alls, or 3) genuinely nice people.

The "lonesome" types have been sitting in their shops all day by themselves and need some sort of human contact. They will talk about anything, from their children to the weather, to keep you from leaving after your sales call has been completed.

The "know-it-alls" are accounts that love to purvey rumors and criticize all their vendors about the policies and procedures they use to run their businesses. Generally, when asked how they would do things, the know-it-all will either unleash an hour-long dissertation on how they would indeed do it, or simply skirt the issue because they truly don't have a better way. They just want to complain about it. Specifics are not their forte, but generalities are.

The final group consists of just plain good folks. They are great conversationalists, interesting, and enjoy people. Even you don't want to leave these conversations, but time is money. How do you get out gracefully without being rude?

Pre-planning the call prior to going in the shop is the best remedy. Have a good idea about what objectives you want to accomplish in the call and a specific time frame for meeting those goals, before you enter the front door. When you first see your account, tell them the reasons for your sales call and how much time you expect it to take. You can also casually mention that your next appointment is at a certain time. This tells the customer three important things:

1. The reason you are there and what you expect from the sales call.
2. How much time you have allocated to the call.
3. You have to be somewhere else at a certain time, so they can't talk your ear off.

Even this approach will not work with some accounts, but at least you will know you made a good attempt at not wasting a big part of your day with just one account. If you do get caught in a long call you can't escape, try to write a large order. It will do a great deal for your disposition as you leave the account after that three or four hour sales call.

SELLING IS NOT TELLING

I regret often that I have spoken; never that I have been silent.
- Syrus

Once when I was sitting in a sales training course, the leader asked everyone to list his or her three biggest issues in the field. He started to go around the room asking for everyone's issues. When he got half way around the room, he stopped and turned to one of the guys sitting on the other side of the room and said "Tell me what his three issues were." This poor guy couldn't remember a single issue that the person had presented. He was embarrassed, and this little exercise really set the tone for the entire meeting. Listening was paramount if we wanted to be successful in life or in the field.

As a sales manager and trainer, one great thing about the job is that there is never a lack of conversation. Salespeople love to talk. I once traveled with a guy who hummed constantly. He didn't even know that he was doing it. When I brought it to his attention, he was shocked. It had become a habit many years ago and he couldn't even remember when he started. Another guy was a whistler, but we won't go into that. The point here is that silence is filled with something in a sales call, and usually it is the salesperson talking to fill that silence.

Does it make you uncomfortable to have silence during a sales call? My answer here is: sometimes. There is nothing worse than a salesperson walking into a shop, introducing him or herself, and then standing there waiting for the customer to make the next move. I have actually seen customers make that well-known rolling hands move to the salesperson to say "Come on, now. What's next?" It's pretty bad to think your sales call is going to be driven by your good looks. Silence is very appropriate when you have asked a question and you're waiting for a response. Typically, the salesperson will jump right in if there is a break and answer their own question. We have to remember that customers sometimes need time to think about their answer. Nine times out of ten, their answer is going to be different from what you thought it might be.

A monologue is not a sales call. It is a sermon. Very few customers or prospects like to be preached to during business hours. Ask questions and give the customer a chance to respond. You might be surprised at what they will tell you. Selling is not telling.

Turning Spectators into Participants

My grandmother started walking five miles a day when she was sixty.
She's ninety-five now, and we don't know where the hell she is.
- Ellen DeGeneres

Did you ever have a consumer walk in on you while you were making a presentation to a client? Most of us grumble about the interruption that occurs in the sales call. The nerve of somebody coming into the client's shop and wanting to purchase something. How rude! Well, like it or not, these consumers are our life blood and if they don't come through that door, your account will be out of business very quickly.

In years past when I was actually on the road selling, I always tried to bring the consumer into the selling process. Many times when the client was busy with something else, I would take the opportunity to speak with the other person waiting and perhaps even show them some of my wares. It would usually open up a conversation about my company, the types of products that I was showing, availability, trends etc. More often than not, the person that I took the time to work with would end up purchasing one of my products versus one from the competition.

It was easy when I turned the spectator into a participant by making them part of the sales call. The client appreciated it because they were busy with other customers and didn't want the one left unattended to walk out the door. They even appreciated the opportunity to work with my products which translated into a sale for me.

Another thing that happens regularly is that a person is called out of the back room to participate in the selection process. They usually like to sit back until they are engaged and brought into the conversation. In many cases, they can play a very big part in determining your success with the account. Make sure they are treated as though they are important, because they are.

If your sales call gets interrupted, or others are brought into the selection process, your presentation should expand to include anyone who shows an interest in your products. Make sure the opportunity doesn't pass you by.

CHARACTERISTICS OF A SUCCESSFUL SALESPERSON

IT IS ALL IN HOW YOU APPROACH IT

*Knowledge comes, but wisdom lingers. It may not be difficult to store up in
the mind a vast quantity of facts within a comparatively short time,
but the ability to form judgements requires the severe discipline of hard work
and the tempering heat of experience and maturity.*
- Calvin Coolidge

Have you ever come out of a sales call and wondered
why you didn't get the order? What made the conversation
change direction on you? How did you lose control of the
sales call? Was your approach changed by the customer
without you even realizing it? Many calls end in frustration simply because the approach wasn't planned and well
thought-out.

I have had salespeople ask me why I think a call went
the wrong way and really, every situation is different. The
one thing all calls have in common is that the individual
approach can be as varied as the salesperson or the customer. The trick is finding the right approach that fits that
salesperson, that customer, and the final objective the
salesperson has set for the call.

So, the sales call is going great right up until the time
when the customer hits you with an unanticipated objection that you hadn't planned to deal with. Most sales calls
can be considered somewhat linear: Point A leads to Point
B, which leads to Point C and so on. Your approach may
have to change if the customer skips to Point D before B
and C have been covered. My advice is to take another
approach which will allow you to still cover all the points,
not necessarily in sequential order, but still leading to the
final point which hopefully will result in writing the order.

Backing up and taking another approach is not always
the easiest thing to do. It produces a variety of situations

which can be challenging and fun for the salesperson. This is what makes you a professional. Pre-call planning can cover some of these situations, but sometimes it may not cover the unexpected. When this happens, use another plan of attack. It is all in how you approach it.

Quietly Confident

Be courteous to all, but intimate with few; and let those few be well tried before you give them your confidence.
- George Washington

There is nothing more inspiring for a sales manager than to have qualified people working for him who also have confidence. Being self-assured as a person and a professional can quickly translate into increased top line sales. The customer always enjoys dealing with a salesperson that knows what he or she is talking about; it is the salesperson's responsibility to make sure their confidence doesn't become an ego issue.

I once had a competitor described to me by an account as an "egomaniac." I asked her to describe to me her definition of this term. She said the guy only talked about himself and never seemed concerned about her needs as a customer. She went further, saying that he ran down his company by telling her all the problems they had. He said he had set answers for the problems, the company just wouldn't listen to him and make the changes. She was so put off by the salesman that she stopped doing business with the company and went so far as to write the salesman's boss to express her displeasure with the situation.

The salesman had crossed the line from being a confident person to being egotistical. There is nothing wrong with being proud of one's accomplishments. But having to constantly talk about them and reference situations that only concern you quickly become boring for the other person in the conversation. In fact, it is not a conversation at all, it is a monologue.

I attended a seminar last year given by a friend of mine who is in sales consulting. He was going down a list of things or terms that were "in" and those that were "out." At the top of the list was the following:

Out: Me   In: You

People enjoy talking about themselves. If you don't feel this, direct your next conversation away from yourself and ask the person you are speaking with something about them. Watch how the conversation is quickly taken over by the other person. Another good example is to ask any parent about their child or children—there goes 10 minutes at a minimum. No one can resist talking about their children because they are, in most cases, very proud of them.

There are times when talking about yourself is OK. Making yourself the butt of a joke, drawing on work or real life experiences as examples, relating humbly to another person's problem, empathy, and using related work experiences to answer questions; all can prove helpful and provide quiet confidence without involving your ego.

Using "we" instead of "me" is a good way to keep your ego in check. Test yourself next time you make a sales call by counting the number of times you talk emphatically about yourself. If it is more than three times, a little self-analysis should be done. Being confident is a good thing, but having a big ego is not, unless you know how to keep it in check. Do you?

CONTROLLING IMPULSIVENESS IN SALES

Few people think more than two or three times a year. I've made an international reputation for myself by thinking once or twice a week.
- George Bernard Shaw

Ever want to tell a customer to "go take a hike?" Did you do it? Or did you take some time to cool off and then approach the problem from a different perspective? Whichever the case, I am sure you learned some very valuable lessons. An impulse that produces a knee-jerk reaction is not in your best interest. Shock value only works in the movies, it never works in sales.

When I think of impulsiveness, I always think of impulse buying. This is a good thing when we are trying to write an order. Grocery store chains are the kings of providing the opportunity to impulse buy. Checkout lines are full of people who pick up that one last thing that isn't really needed and drop it in their cart. Internet shopping carts are another huge avenue for impulse buying.

When a salesperson is hired for a job, the manager always hopes the company is getting a professional, a person with good credentials who knows how to handle a difficult situation with a large degree of tact and good manners. The manager further hopes that the salesperson is able to handle difficult situations without creating a bigger problem than the one that already exists. It is imperative that salespeople do not act on impulse, which can produce a negative behavior in the customer.

There are occasional situations that require us to back away and approach things from a different viewpoint. Impulse reactions are usually the result of a lack of good planning. If you have taken the time to analyze the customer's needs, personality, and opportunities, you will have already thought out the situation before it occurs. There is no chance to react impulsively. Another thing: most impulse reactions in sales cause a negative situation to occur. Guard against these surprises by planning.

Controlling impulsiveness in sales is a learned trait. If you get into a situation that stretches your patience or one that pushes you beyond normal limits, take a deep breath, back away, and rope-a-dope. Mohammed Ali made this technique famous when he fought Joe Frazier in the Thriller From Manila. This technique when applied to sales allows you to take a breather without doing anything impulsive, then approach the situation from another direction after the customer has calmed down.

Sales calls can change quickly. Be prepared with a variety of responses and don't do anything impulsive you might regret later. Customers are hard to find and its important to keep the ones you've got.

FLEXIBILITY IN SALES

Variety's the very spice of life, that gives it all its flavour.
- Cowper, The Task

If you're in sales, flexibility is important. This is true from many standpoints: your style, your schedule, your itinerary, your approach, or simply your demeanor. All are crucial parts of the sales process. Being flexible means you must be able to handle situations differently, or you have to be able to change quickly in order to accommodate either your customer, your company, your family, or yourself.

Webster's Dictionary has three distinct, yet similar definitions for the word flexible:

- Capable of being bent; easily bent.
- Susceptible of modification or adaptation; adaptable.
- Willing or disposed to yield; pliable.

When was the last time you consciously bent your schedule to accommodate a customer? Have you recently adapted your style to deal with a different personality type? Did you give a bigger discount to make the sale? All of these are examples of flexibility in sales. A rigid person who cannot adapt to the person(s) they are working with or to a difficult sales objection will find it hard to be very good at sales. So many situations in the office and in the field require us to change our approach in order to make the sale happen.

When you deal with a customer, you have three basic types of interaction. You can try to sell them a tangible product. You can try to sell them a tangible service. Or you may try to establish a relationship that is a free intangible. Each one will require some measure of flexibility on your part.

If you will take a moment to think back over the last few months, you will be able to identify many examples of your flexibility. If you can't identify a few, you should examine situations when you were not being flexible, and consider what you could have positively changed by taking another approach. There is no need to bend in every situation, but by knowing when to bend—and how much—your sales, and even your demeanor, will always be improving.

THE ART OF TELLING JOKES

Man alone suffers so excruciatingly in the world
that he was compelled to invent laughter.
- Nietzche, The Will to Power

There is nothing better than getting a good laugh from a customer. Laughter opens up the atmosphere during a sales call, letting the conversation be free-flowing, and in general, more casual. There is nothing that can soften the atmosphere better than a good joke.

Salespeople have always been known for their joke telling ability. I wish I had started documenting jokes I was told when I first started traveling. I could have written several books from the material that I would have by now. As with most people, I enjoy recalling a funny story that can make people laugh. Jokes can be a great way to bridge gaps that exist between you and your customer. On the other hand, a joke can also polarize you from the account and make it difficult to ever regain the comradery that should exist between the salesperson and the customer.

Joke telling is, first of all, an art. The ability to deliver the right voice inflection or have the proper timing with difficult material can make the difference between a good joke teller and a great joke teller. I often wonder where the myriad of material that comes my way finds its beginnings. Somebody has to take the time to write these down or perhaps, only tell them to a friend and thus the daisy-chain starts. If you choose to tell a joke, practice your delivery as you would with any other presentation material.

Audit the material closely. Nothing can be worse than telling an off-color joke to an account. This can harm your reputation, not only with the account, but with your entire account base.

Let the joke or funny story have some tie-in to your sales presentation. A point can be magnified many times if you use a clever tie-in. It also will guarantee that your customer will recall at a later time the point you were trying to make during your presentation.

Use caution when working with a prospective customer. You do not know the prospect well enough to judge if they may find the joke funny or, on the other hand, offensive. Prudence is best in all cases here.

Make sure you interject the story at the proper time. It can easily break your sales call into parts and will get you off track. You may not recover from shifting the conversation away from your products if you bring a joke into the discussion. One joke can lead to another, and another, then another, and before long you have lost time, your presentation, and maybe your sale.

Limit the number of jokes you tell an account. One or two at the most. When salesmen used to travel from one city to another by train or bus in days gone by, they were the common mode of joke movement and funny story telling. In today's marketplace, your accounts expect more from you than just being a source for jokes.

Salespeople have to be very careful in a sales call from many aspects. Your ability to make good judgments about your comments and stories is part of what makes you a professional salesperson. Don't take chances with questionable material. It could cost you more than the sale at hand.

LEARNING NEW TRICKS

*The road to excess leads to the palace of wisdom; for we never know
what is enough until we know what is more than enough.*
- William Blake

You can't teach an old dog new tricks, or can you?
I've been told this over the years by various figures of
authority; but I have never really believed it. You can
teach old dogs new tricks. Tricks for my purposes here are
just habits. Habits can be learned and relearned if the
individual is willing to take the time to work on them.

A few years ago I had to take on the project of
automating a sales force for the first time. It was a difficult project at best. I was somewhat familiar with computers and the many new and different versions of contact
management software. I read books and bought several
different types of computers to help me adjust to the learning curve in technology. I soon found that I had only
brushed the surface of what has become a long, sometimes
frustrating, but always enjoyable journey in the world of
cyberspace.

Once I had brought myself, an old dog by every
account, up to a point where I felt a small level of confidence in sales automation, I proceeded to work out an
experimental program for my sales force. I had a myriad
of personalities, levels of computer skills, and all ages to
deal with in this project. Some were so-called "computer
literate," others did not know what a mouse was. To make
a long story short, the project took a great deal of time to
implement because we had to teach many old dogs new
tricks. I am happy to report that today, every person who

started in that project is active in cyberspace daily. Many have taken to the computer and now use it as a part of their daily routine.

Another example is my father. I pushed him into buying a computer a few years back. Now, this guy had only rotary phones in his home until 1997. You can't imagine my level of frustration when I visited my parents and had to use a tone dialer to retrieve messages. Well, since my Dad bought a computer, he is now actively communicating with family members via daily e-mail, researching family genealogy, and has written five books. Not bad for an old dog that took the time to learn a few new tricks.

When attempting something new, follow a few simple rules:

- Be willing to give it a try.
- Practice every chance you get.
- Never stop asking if there is a better way.
- Re-evaluate regularly.

It's great to see old dogs learn new things, particularly since I am now one of those old dogs.

Polishing Your Image

She wears her clothes as if they were thrown on her with a pitchfork.
- Swift, Polite Conversation

Image can be a salesperson's best friend or worst nightmare. Your image is sometimes formed slowly over a period of years, but it can also be formed quickly. Both can work in your favor with your account. Image should be a guarded possession and it should be polished occasionally. It doesn't take much to change your image. If you don't believe me, listen to what your accounts say about other salespeople who call on them. One push too hard in the wrong direction, one joke told in poor taste, one broken promise, any of these can have a permanent impact on your professional image.

Salespeople often get into ruts. This can happen for a variety of reasons. Your image can get into a rut with your accounts, your manager, your favorite CSR (customer service rep.) If you feel your image needs a little polishing, try a few of the following suggestions and check out the difference it makes.

- Use breath mints.
- Carry a new briefcase.
- Starch your shirts.
- Shine your shoes.
- Tell a funny story and relate it to your sales presentation.
- Have reports handy, with numbers to refer to, during the call.

- Sneeze in the opposite direction from your sample case.
- Purposely lock your keys in your car to get to know your account better.

Seriously, there is no substitute for dressing in good taste and having proper hygiene. You can be as flamboyant as you want or as conservative as you want in the way you dress at home. But dressing tastefully for work is a must to maintain the proper image. You can polish it even more by dressing up. Ties can always come off, but you can't put one on if don't have one with you.

Customers remember what you say and do. Your image in their eyes is directly proportional to the integrity of your words and actions. Critique yourself every now and then. Your image in the customer's eyes is just as important as the product you are selling. Always guard it and polish it regularly. It will pay big dividends.

Hearing the Right Answers

The answer my friend is blowing in the wind,
the answer is blowing in the wind.
- Joan Baez

One of the most difficult parts of the sales call is waiting for the customer to answer your questions. Most salespeople have the tendency to ask a question and, when the account wants to take a minute to formulate the answer, become impatient. The salesperson wants to jump right in and answer the question.

Taking the time to quietly wait for a response to a question is a learned art. The normal tendency is to "help" the customer formulate their answer. If we learn to wait, the answer may sometimes be the same as we thought; many times it is not. We unintentionally lead the conversation to our way of thinking without really knowing where the client stands on the subject. This can be frustrating for the customer and will prevent the salesperson from truly uncovering needs and potential opportunities.

Sales calls need to have time to develop. Learning to listen allows for that time. Good listeners are better salespeople. There are numerous articles and books about being a good listener, so I won't try to redevelop that topic here. Just remember that listening, waiting for the response, will allow you to hear the right answers—if time was taken to formulate the right questions. One dictates the other.

Good listening skills and good questioning skills will bring you a bit closer to hearing the right answers from your customer. This may not always yield the answer you want to hear. It will, however, give you a better chance to position your conversation during your sales call. By directing the conversation, you are in control. It is a very powerful tool for getting to hear the right answers.

Voice Tone

Results! Why, man, I have gotten a lot of results.
I know several thousand things that won't work.
- Thomas A. Edison

Have you ever been told that you give bad phone? I once sat in a customer service seminar and listened to several people saying the same thing over a speakerphone. The audience was not allowed to see who was doing the talking. When the exercise was over, the audience got to rate each caller and try to match up the voice with the face. I blew it on every account. It might have been different if I'd had previous conversations with the people involved in the seminar, but this exercise proved to me you should never take for granted your voice tone when speaking, either on the phone or in person.

One of the hints I learned at the seminar mentioned above is that the person on the other end of the phone needs to "hear" you smiling through the phone line. The leader suggested a small mirror on the desk by the phone would help remind us to smile. If people remember to smile while talking on the phone, it helps them to come across as happy and helpful.

Another suggestion is to record yourself to actually hear how you sound. What an eye (and ear) opener! You get to hear exactly what your customers are hearing. If you sound good, you are probably doing fine when speaking to customers. If you have little inflection in your voice, sound bored, speak too loudly or too softly, you are probably giving bad phone.

Make sure you get off to a good start with each call.

The mood of the person on the other end of the phone comes through with the very first "hello." Here is where planning what to say becomes important. Sounding good is essential, but it really doesn't make any difference how good you sound if what you say isn't worth hearing.

Prepare what you are going to say and practice saying it with the proper tone of voice. Your customer will hear your smile no matter what the distance.

A Salesperson's Personal Concerns

COFFEE TIME

Jane Hathaway: Chief, haven't you ever heard of the saying
"It's not whether you win or lose, it's how you play the game?"
Mr. Drysdale: Yes, I've heard it. And I consider it one of the
most ridiculous statements ever made.
- The Beverly Hillbillies

I used to have a boss who started every conversation with "Let's go get a cup of coffee." He was in general a pretty wired guy anyway, but as the day went on every meeting became more intense thanks to him being over-caffeinated.

A few years ago my doctor recommended that I get off of caffeine altogether for blood pressure reasons. He said "You can either do this on your own or you will be drooling on your ties watching your children grow up." I took his advice and went cold turkey off the caffeine. I had headaches for two weeks and swore that once this ordeal was over, I would never get back on the stuff. Well, as time went on, I slowly went back to the coffee. Today, I still don't drink as much coffee as I use to, but I do enjoy that morning cup of Joe.

When I was on the road full-time, I always enjoyed the social time of having a cup of coffee with my customers. I always took it black because I didn't want to be a bother to the customer. I have since given up that effort and now I ask for it just the way I really like it. The customer is usually very accommodating.

My favorite memory of coffee time was with an account in Texas who will remain nameless. He would always schedule salespeople to come in first thing in the morning, then he'd ask if you wanted some coffee. When the piping cup of Java showed up, it was loaded with

brandy and cream, "Just enough," he said "to get you through till lunch." Well, that day was shot, because you can't call on customers with breath like that. So I had a second cup, and I made it very clear that in order for me to have a second, I would need an order—because I wasn't going to be able to see anybody else that day thanks to his "special" coffee. I knew after that to find out in advance what was going to be in my coffee.

You can make a great impression and learn a great deal about your customers during coffee time. Bringing in some doughnuts is always a nice touch, to treat the customer and the staff. They don't forget these types of gestures. I will make one recommendation, speaking from experience: don't be shy about asking to use the facilities before you leave. It could be a long way to your next call. That was always the case in Texas.

DINING SOLO

Give us this day our daily bread.
- Matthew, Chapter VI, Verse 2

When we speak of road hazards, most of us usually think of potholes or drunk drivers. Not many people think about the issue of dining alone. When the maitre-d' looks at you and says "Just one?" chances are you, like most of us, feel the quick uneasiness associated with dining alone.

A 1997 Travel Industry Association survey indicated that 207 million US residents made business trips during the year. 71% of those trips were made by people that were alone. There is actually a web site devoted to this issue now, www.solodining.com. It will provide you with a list of restaurants in 29 states, which cater to people who will be eating alone.

The author of the web site, Marya Charles Alexander, offers a few tips that I thought might come in handy for those of us who are exposed to this situation on a regular basis. Even though the tips seem to be more for upscale dining establishments and not for take-out eat-in your-room Kentucky Fried Chicken, they offer some advice that can help us deal with a sometimes difficult situation.

The web site hits these high points:
- Try to make your dining alone experience a familiar one, by trying breakfast or lunch in your hometown first.
- Dine early. The waiters are less likely to see you as an inconvenience and a small tip (as opposed to the more

profitable tables of couples or groups.

- Avoid candlelight restaurants that cater to couples. Apparently, people like to stare at people eating alone in these types of settings.
- Call ahead. Let them know you will be dining alone and request a table that is out of the way.
- Make lunch your big meal of the day. That way you won't have to sit alone in a restaurant at night when other people have dining partners.

DOING WITHOUT

The wise man thinks about his troubles only when there is some purpose in doing so; at other times he thinks about other things.
- Bertrand Russell

I was reading an article the other day about the State of Massachusetts changing its employee paychecks to a bi-weekly system. This had created a variety of different circumstances for the employees, all of whom handled their money differently. Some of the employees were caught off guard and had no money for that week. Others were prepared and didn't have to worry about the change in the pay schedule.

I found this to be interesting in that companies also learn how to function differently when cash flow is tight. Employees must become more inventive and resourceful during these times. Policies and procedures can be tightened to accommodate a tight financial situation. Cuts are made when they have to be, while other areas are expanded to keep the company on track, ready for the internal situation to change. The lessons learned during these times are hard. But if these lessons are applied when times are good, the company will grow and prosper beyond its wildest imagination.

During tough times, doing without is a regular occurrence. My grandfather used to call it "character building." I didn't really understand this until later in life, but character building is the best way to approach difficult times and is the best method of preparing for the good times ahead. If you can look for ways to keep extra money in your pocket when times are tough, it will come back to benefit you many times over in the future when times are good.

The lesson is tough when you first have to learn it. But by embracing it, you will appreciate the good times even more. Our attitude tells the story. Why complain about something you can't control? Take a positive approach and do without something once in a while. You will be amazed at your resourcefulness and how good it feels to keep the situation in perspective and control. Lessons learned today from doing without will be a huge benefit to you tomorrow when you have more than you need.

Epilogue

Management vs Sales

A man is flying in a hot air balloon and realizes he is lost. He reduces height and spots a man down below. He lowers the balloon further and shouts: "Excuse me, can you tell me where I am?"

The salesman below says "Yes, you're in a hot air balloon, hovering 30 feet above this field."

"You must work in Sales" says the balloonist.

"I do" replies the salesman. "How did you know?"

"Well" says the balloonist, "everything you have told me is technically correct, but it's no use to anyone."

The salesman below says "You must work in Management."

"I do" replies the balloonist, "but how did you know?"

"Well," says the salesman, "you don't know where you are, or where you're going, but you expect me to be able to help. You're in the same position you were before we met, but now it's my fault!"

About the Author

A veteran of the picture framing industry for over 25 years, Larry Bauman has experienced all aspects of the industry. He worked his way through high school and college managing a retail picture frame shop. After graduating from Emory University, he accepted a sales position with Piedmont Moulding until 1981. He joined Clark Moulding as Executive Vice-President until 1988. His experience working with domestic and international distribution took him to Crescent Cardboard as Vice-President of Sales in 1988. Bauman remained at Crescent until 1998, when he joined The Williamson Company as Vice-President of Sales and Marketing. He worked as a contracted consultant for them until June of 2000, at which time he decided to pursue his own business interests by opening Phoenix Business Consulting. Phoenix specializes in the framing industry, providing strategic planning, special projects, product sourcing, sales training and automation to a diverse client base. Additional information may be obtained at: www.phoenixbusinessconsulting.com. Bauman is the author of a bi-weekly newsletter, and is currently working on his second book.